"I'm so excited for the power and encouragement that *Sundays at the Track* will bring to people's hearts. It's beautiful to see how many souls have discovered the truth and freedom that go far beyond competition on the track. I'm so grateful that these powerful stories have been jam-packed into one awesome read!"

Matt DiBenedetto, NASCAR driver

"*Sundays at the Track* is a testament to how faith and God's will have powered some of the most remarkable moments at the track and have helped in overcoming some of our greatest challenges as drivers, owners, team members, and others within the industry. I was honored to share the important piece that Jesus has played in both my personal and professional life paths in hopes of inspiring others. These stories about the role of faith in pushing us to life's finish line are a must-read for any NASCAR fan."

Chase Briscoe, NASCAR driver

"Lee does a great job pulling the reader into these inspiring stories of faith from folks in NASCAR who are often viewed as larger than life. Seeing the intensity with which they live life in motorsports competition and knowing that Jesus our Lord and Savior is a part of their journey humanizes them in ways anyone can relate to. As believers, we are called to spread God's Word and live in His ways, and connecting with everyday stories of sports heroes allows us to strengthen our own faith for our everyday lives."

Kelley Earnhardt Miller, CEO of JR Motorsports

"Lee has done a great job of capturing many stories from within our sport that serve as testaments to the power of faith and remind us that even in the fastest of moments, God is always present, guiding us toward the ultimate finish line. *Sundays at the Track* isn't just for racing enthusiasts; it's for anyone seeking inspiration and spiritual encouragement."

Michael McDowell, 2021 Daytona 500 Champion

"When it comes to NASCAR, most of us think of speed, power, and precision. In *Sundays at the Track*, we're reminded God sometimes has to slow us down in order to show us who's really behind the wheel. Lee's stories reveal how God's grace and faithfulness have turned around the lives of some of your favorite stock car personalities."

Jim Daly, president of Focus on the Family

"Through highs and lows, good times and bad, wins and losses, the most successful athletes and those that surround them have the determination and focus to never give up. However, the highs, good times, and wins never bring lasting joy and true peace. In the pages of this book you will read stories of many from the world of NASCAR who have discovered lasting joy and peace in all circumstances, good and bad, and where they found it—or, more specifically, in whom they found it. His name is Jesus."

Billy Mauldin, president and senior chaplain
of Motor Racing Outreach

"*Sundays at the Track* brings some of the most honest, inspirational stories from the shadows of the racing community into the light of God's grace and faithfulness."

David Pierce, chief media officer of K-LOVE

"In this book, you will learn that there is a lot more to the NASCAR community than going fast in circles. Although these individuals are blessed to do what they love, not everything in their world is glitzy, glamorous, or perfect. They too have to struggle and meet the daily challenges of life that we all face. And for many of them, their faith in Christ Jesus is their anchor through it all."

Stevie Waltrip, wife of NASCAR Hall
of Fame driver Darrell Waltrip

"*Sundays at the Track* is perfect for motorsports fans or anyone who might be searching or struggling with their faith.

Throughout this amazing book, all different personalities from the world of NASCAR share personal stories and insights about God's faithfulness!"

Larry McReynolds, broadcast analyst
for NASCAR on FOX

"NASCAR is one of the most loved sports in America, and if you're a fan, you know endless stats on your favorite driver and team. But have you ever wanted a peek behind the curtain to meet some of the wonderful people that pour their hearts and souls into making NASCAR into something we can't get enough of? If so, then *Sundays at the Track* is just what you've been waiting for."

Susan Chastain, mother of NASCAR
Cup Series driver Ross Chastain

"*Sundays at the Track* shows that there are more important things than trophies and bent race cars. Through the highest of highs and the lowest of lows, your faith in Jesus can and will sustain you. Nobody can do it alone, and I'm so thankful we don't have to."

Phil Parsons, broadcast analyst
for NASCAR on FOX

For those of us who love motorsports, *Sundays at the Track* reveals the spiritual battle going on inside every driver and team member in the midst of their pressure to win the race that will impact their lives and the lives of those they influence—for eternity!

Barry Meguiar, third-generation leader of Meguiar's Car
Wax and host of *Car Crazy TV* for 18 years

SUNDAYS AT THE TRACK

SUNDAYS AT THE TRACK

INSPIRING TRUE STORIES OF FAITH, LEADERSHIP, AND DETERMINATION FROM THE WORLD OF NASCAR

LEE WEEKS

Revell

a division of Baker Publishing Group
Grand Rapids, Michigan

© 2024 by Lee Weeks

Published by Revell
a division of Baker Publishing Group
Grand Rapids, Michigan
RevellBooks.com

Printed in the United States of America

Library of Congress Cataloging-in-Publication Data
Names: Weeks, Lee, 1970– author.
Title: Sundays at the track : inspiring true stories of faith, leadership, and
    determination from the world of NASCAR / Lee Weeks.
Description: Grand Rapids, Michigan : Revell, a division of Baker Publishing
    Group, 2024. | Includes bibliographical references.
Identifiers: LCCN 2024014224 | ISBN 9780800745547 (cloth) | ISBN 9781493447275
    (ebook)
Subjects: LCSH: Automobile racing drivers—United States—Biography. |
    Automobile racing drivers—Religious life—United States. | Automobile racing
    managers—United States—Biography. | Automobile racing managers—
    Religious life—United States. | Automobile racing—Religious aspects—
    Christianity. | NASCAR (Association)
Classification: LCC GV1032.A1 W44 2024 | DDC 796.72092/273 [B]—dc23/
    eng/20240411
LC record available at https://lccn.loc.gov/2024014224

Cover design by David Carlson, Studio Gearbox

Baker Publishing Group publications use paper produced from sustainable forestry practices and postconsumer waste whenever possible.

24 25 26 27 28 29 30   7 6 5 4 3 2 1

CONTENTS

Contents

Contents

FOREWORD

Welcome to *Sundays at the Track*, where we share more with you than most people ever get to know about our NASCAR family!

When my wife and I helped found Motor Racing Outreach in the 1980s, we never dreamed it would turn out to be the ministry it is in NASCAR today. For over 35 years MRO's presence has been impacting lives as, week in and week out, they allow the Holy Spirit to work through them, blessing, teaching, and encouraging men, women, and children of all ages as they discover and seek to grow in their own faith in God. What began as a small Bible study group meeting in a hotel room on Friday nights has evolved into an instrumental part of the day-to-day world of NASCAR, with chapel services on race day, baptisms, Bible club for children, and much more. The biggest compliment we have ever received is to be referred to as the people who are "the glue that holds NASCAR together."

Sundays at the Track is a compilation of stories that share about this impact and the personal faith of many of NASCAR's biggest names, as well as a few names you may be less familiar with. Each chapter in the book is a testimony of God's unconditional love, grace, and mercy. God's faithfulness is the common denominator in each of these personal stories as He chases and relentlessly pursues each individual. In any race, there is a lead driver everyone is chasing; but in life, God is the Lead Driver, and He is chasing us. The goal is that we may know Him personally and grow daily in our relationship with Him. The win is eternity in His presence. The trophy is His peace and His unconditional love that passes all understanding as we daily run the race in our own lives.

As you read through these stories and see for yourself the impact God has had on the lives of our community, Stevie and I hope and pray that you too will be impacted, encouraged, challenged, and equipped to know Him and pursue Him just as He has pursued and caught us!

Blessings,

Darrell Waltrip, three-time NASCAR Cup Series champion

INTRODUCTION

NASCAR is a paradoxical sport—part sprint, part marathon. A 2.5-mile oval track becomes 500 miles to the finish line. Most drivers will tell you that stock car racing is all about speed. But the racecar that has the fastest qualifying lap and secures the pole position to start the race isn't always the first to cross the finish line. The time between the wave of the green flag and the checkered flag in a Cup Series race is a fleeting window of opportunity for the nearly 40 drivers who flip the ignition switch to start their engines. Diagnostic data, mechanics, aerodynamics, race strategy, pit stop efficiency, and steering clear of a collision often determine where a race team finishes—or doesn't.

Competition can seem more like a war of attrition when maneuvering a 3,400-pound machine at 200 miles per hour amid five-wide racing, as drivers try to dodge that cataclysmic crash bent on wrecking their chances of finding victory lane.

Go. Wait. Change lanes. Accelerate. Slow down. Pursue. Push. Pass. Pit. Split-second decision-making on the racetrack can be the difference between success and failure.

On so many levels, racing the superspeedways, short tracks, ovals, and road courses can be a metaphor for the race called life. Every day, week, month, and year, most of us are chasing something, right? Deadlines. Obligations. Goals. Dreams. Success. Relationships. Acceptance. Respect. Love. And like motor racing, all these pursuits take time.

Time ranks up there with precious commodities like air and water. Sometimes it seems there's never enough of it to spend with family and friends or to do all that we need or want to do. Time on earth is priceless but often wasted. Time is always of the essence because it can't be replaced. The psalmist writes in Scripture, "So teach us to number our days that we may get a heart of wisdom" (Ps. 90:12). In the world of NASCAR, race teams are always striving to shave a hundredth of a second off their lap qualifying times or pit stops. Changing two tires or all four at strategic times throughout the race can make a racecar faster than competitors with worn tires trying to hold their position on a slick track. Talk about a race against time.

Then there are the eyes in the sky that every race team depends on—the spotter who perches high above the grandstands and is equipped with high-powered binoculars and a two-way radio with direct communication to the driver and crew chief. The spotter's job is to constantly communicate what is unfolding on the track ahead of, beside, and, when necessary, behind their driver. The spotter's vantage point enables them to see the entire race unfold before their eyes. The spotter can tell the driver whether the inside or outside lanes seem to have the most momentum and what turn angle is necessary to avoid clipping or getting passed by an approaching racecar. Then, when the big one happens—that crash on the superspeedway that collects nearly half the racecars in a heap of mangled metal—it's the spotter who guides the lucky driver unscathed through the smoke and mayhem.

Fortunately, in the race of life we have a Spotter who is perfectly capable of guiding us through everything we face. His vision is flawless. He knows the beginning from the end and everything in between. He is our Creator. He is never surprised or caught unaware by what comes our way, and He has the perfect plan to lead us to victory. Hebrews 12:1–3 offers timeless teaching from God's Word about how to be victorious in the race called life:

> Therefore, since we are surrounded by so great a cloud of witnesses, let us also lay aside every weight, and sin which clings so closely, and let us run with endurance the race that is set before us, looking to Jesus, the founder and perfecter of our faith, who for the joy that was set before him endured the cross, despising the shame, and is seated at the right hand of the throne of God. Consider him who endured from sinners such hostility against himself, so that you may not grow weary or fainthearted.

In this book, you'll read stories about how some of the most successful people in NASCAR have endured all sorts of trials and discovered Jesus to be more than faithful in their daily lives. Hopefully, these real-life stories of faith from on and off the track will inspire you with practical biblical insights about how to persevere and overcome trials en route to experiencing God's best for your life.

Joe Gibbs

When God Doesn't Make Sense

IN PROFESSIONAL SPORTS, the name Joe Gibbs is synonymous with winning. Joe has reached the pinnacle of success three times as a Super Bowl champion head football coach. Five times he has hoisted the NASCAR Cup championship trophy as a team owner. His career accolades—in not just one but two professional sports—have landed him in the Halls of Fame among the greatest ever to compete in the National Football League and the NASCAR Cup Series.

As head football coach of the Washington Redskins, Joe's career spanned three decades, and his teams made four Super Bowl appearances in the 1980s and early 1990s. During his tenure, the Redskins won 10 or more games nine times and recorded only three losing seasons. In 16 seasons at the helm of one of the most storied franchises in the history of professional sports, Joe amassed 171 victories, including a career 17-7 record in the playoffs. He is also the only Super Bowl champion head coach to be victorious with three different starting quarterbacks—Joe Theismann (1983), Doug Williams (1988), and Mark Rypien (1992), none of whom are in the Hall of Fame.

And since 2000, Joe Gibbs Racing has won five NASCAR Cup Series championships with drivers Bobby Labonte (2000), Tony Stewart (2002, 2005), and Kyle Busch (2015, 2019). JGR has also claimed four Xfinity Series titles (2009, 2016, 2021, 2022), which included Joe's grandson, Ty Gibbs, in the driver's seat.

For all of his legendary achievements on the gridiron and racetrack, Joe readily gives God the credit, followed by an assembly of elite team members. In addition to his record-setting success throughout his professional sports career, Joe has also experienced gut-wrenching loss in the game of life. More recently, in the span of three years, both of Joe's sons, his only children, died less than a year before their 50th birthdays.

Joe's oldest son, J.D., cofounded JGR with his father in 1992 after Joe finished his first coaching stint with the Redskins. J.D., who served as JGR's longtime president, died January 11, 2019, after battling a degenerative brain disease for five years. Then, on November 6, 2022, Joe's second son, Coy, vice chair of JGR, died in his sleep just hours after his son Ty won the Xfinity Series championship.

"It is the greatest heartbreak, I believe, that someone can experience," Joe says. "But the thing that is great about what I know about my boys is that both of them had given their life to Christ at an early age. Consequently, I get to spend eternity with them forever. God's Word says that our life here on earth, if you think about it, it's so short that we can't compare that with God's eternal glory. And glory is forever, so I get to be with an all-powerful, all-knowing, all-loving God who has saved me and my boys."

While Joe continues to grieve the loss of his sons, he is equally grateful that Pat, his wife of nearly 60 years, their two daughters-in-law, Melissa and Heather, and their eight grandchildren also profess faith in Jesus Christ as their Savior and Lord. Joe admits that he doesn't understand why his two sons' days on earth ended before his. Nevertheless, he has an inexplicable peace knowing that he will see them again when he trades this world for heaven. "I have a confidence of knowing where I'm going, and I know where my boys are. At some point, I'll join them. That's an exciting thing for me. And I get to spend eternity with them because we've got an all-powerful God who made heaven. So it's going to be so exciting for all of us."

As a college and professional football coach for more than 30 years and a NASCAR team owner since the early 90s, Joe has distinguished himself in both professional sports through relentless preparation and painstaking attention to detail. In the *New York Times* bestseller *Game Plan for Life*, Joe writes, "Whether it's NASCAR, the NFL, or life, when you're playing to win, you have a game plan. If you're serious about winning, nothing—I mean *nothing*—is left to chance."[1]

But when JGR's Denny Hamlin drove the FedEx Toyota to victory lane in the 2019 Daytona 500, the achievement was surreal. It had been barely a month since J.D. had succumbed to a cruel neurological disease, leaving behind his wife and four sons, parents, brother, and race team, who had all thrived under his selfless leadership and godly example. At Lap 170, Hamlin took his first lead in the race. On the roof of his car was written the name J.D. Gibbs. The clean air at the front of the pack allowed the No. 11 car—which was J.D.'s high school and college football jersey number—to showcase its dominating speed on the track. Hamlin led 30 of the final 38 laps en route to capturing the checkered flag, while JGR teammates Kyle Busch and Erik Jones finished second and third respectively. It was the first time since 1997 that teammates finished first, second, and third in the Daytona 500.

What were the chances that the first race following the death of JGR's president—and the Super Bowl of NASCAR, no less—would be won by the driver J.D. had recruited? "I think God's hand was on the race," Joe said in a postrace interview. "Most people, myself included, believe that J.D. had the best seat in the house. It was the greatest victory I've been a part of. We hope that it honored the Lord with everything that took place there."[2]

Citing Psalm 139 as his favorite Scripture passage, Joe says that the psalmist's view of God's heart for people gives him everlasting hope, especially when life doesn't make sense or seem fair. Like when God calls your two sons to their eternal home in heaven while they're still in the prime of their lives and raising godly families. Or when your wife experiences facial paralysis following the surgical removal of a benign tumor from behind her ear. Or when your two-year-old grandson is diagnosed with leukemia and three years later is declared cancer-free. Through it all, Joe's faith in God has held strong like a tree whose roots run deep. When the strong winds blow, the tree bends but doesn't break. Similarly, although Joe has questioned God's actions at times, he's never wavered in his faith that God is always working to bring good out of everything for those who love Him and seek His purposes (Rom. 8:28).

But because God's ways are often different from what we want, and His thoughts are higher than ours, Joe says it's only natural for people to question God when things don't go their way. He admits that he's had to work through his own questions: *Why didn't God show up? Are we just living a life of chance? Why do Christians suffer? Why do some Christians suffer more than others? Do we really reap what we sow?* And again, it's the Bible, God's perfect Word, where Joe finds the answers to life's toughest questions.

> O LORD, you have searched me and known me!
> You know when I sit down and when I rise up;
>   you discern my thoughts from afar.
> You search out my path and my lying down
>   and are acquainted with all my ways.
> Even before a word is on my tongue,
>   behold, O LORD, you know it altogether.
> You hem me in, behind and before,
>   and lay your hand upon me.
> Such knowledge is too wonderful for me;
>   it is high; I cannot attain it. . . .
> Your eyes saw my unformed substance;
> in your book were written, every one of them,
>   the days that were formed for me,
>   when as yet there was none of them. (Ps. 139:1–6, 16)

Joe says he's convinced that J.D. and Coy lived the exact number of days that God purposed and planned for them. And he is beyond grateful that they were ready to receive their heavenly reward when their Creator called them home. Yet, while Joe continues to grieve his sons' deaths, he holds on to the truth of God's Word in Romans 8:16–18:

> The Spirit himself bears witness with our spirit that we are children of God, and if children, then heirs—heirs of God and fellow heirs with Christ, provided we suffer with him in order that we may also be glorified with him. For I consider that the sufferings of this present time are not worth comparing with the glory that is to be revealed to us.

While game planning and tireless preparation have proven to be Joe's winning formula throughout his professional sports career, he's been equally passionate about helping people make sure that they are prepared for a glorious eternity in heaven. That's why he's poured his life into prison ministry and programs to help troubled youth discover God's purpose for their lives. "The most important decision I ever made was asking Christ to come into my life at nine years old," Joe says. "I wanted to be on His team, and I asked Him to forgive me of my sins and be my Lord and personal Savior. That was the single biggest decision I've ever made because it helps direct every other decision you make in life. And so, it's great knowing that you got God to call on and ask to help you with all the decisions you're making as you go forward in life."

Now in his early 80s, Joe's competitive fire is eclipsed only by his heartfelt responsibility and conviction to strive daily to glorify God and point others to Him. Joe says, "Once we've given our life to Christ, He empowers us to be a witness, and a testimony for Him, as a member of God's team. And wherever you are, or whatever your occupation is, or whatever your age is, God empowers us to be a witness and a testimony for Him. And so, I believe that and I think that's an obligation for all of us. No matter what your walk is in life, there's people that you're around, and whether it's family, whether it's friends, whether it's business partners or teammates, then people are going to be looking at you if you've given your life to Christ. And I think the way you live and your testimony can be a part of bringing people closer to making that decision to follow Christ."

Darrell and Stevie Waltrip

The Marriage Miracle

"**BOOGITY! BOOGITY! BOOGITY!** Let's go racing, boys!"

Darrell Waltrip's spirited proclamation from the NASCAR on FOX broadcast booth ignited the passion of millions of stock car racing fans for nearly two decades. But Waltrip's mantra wasn't just show business. From the time he caught the racing bug at age 6 standing alongside his grandmother in the grandstands at the local dirt track until he retired in 2019 as TV's premiere stock car racing analyst, it's how he lived his life.

Growing up in Owensboro, Kentucky, the oldest son of blue-collar parents, Darrell did most things faster than others—from racing go-karts as a teenager to running the half-mile on the high school track team to late model dirt track racing.

Darrell never questioned what he wanted to do for a living. From the first time he sat in a go-kart, he says, "I felt it in my butt, and that's how you drive by the seat of your pants."

Darrell's full-speed-ahead mentality landed him in law enforcement's sights more than once, including the time they foiled his attempt to drag race in his '69 Chevelle SS, with a 375-horsepower engine and factory-installed chambered exhaust, and the time he was driving too fast on curvy country roads and leveled a young family's swing set in the middle of the night. Fortunately, no one ever got hurt, and his grandfather, who was a sheriff's deputy, always made sure Darrell took responsibility for his actions and made things right. Even after Darrell flipped his Chevelle and landed upside down in his girlfriend Stevie's front yard while successfully eluding police, she still agreed to marry him less than a year after their first date, much to her parents' dismay. She was 19 and he was 23. "We got married for the wrong reasons," Stevie says. "We were too young. We needed to grow up." The couple celebrates their 55th anniversary in 2024.

Darrell began stock car racing at age 16 with a 1936 Chevrolet coupe that he and his father souped up. Soon he was racing late model cars at the speedway in Nashville, Tennessee, and winning a lot. In 1972, he made his NASCAR Cup Series debut at age 25 in his makeshift Mercury. Five races that year grew to 19 in 1973 and another 16 in 1974. By the time Darrell went full-time in 1975, his independent team had already garnered a pole, nine top fives, and 19 top tens in 40 starts. His first Cup victory came that same year at the Nashville Fairgrounds Speedway, the same track where he honed his skills as an amateur.

Darrell showcased the Gatorade colors on cars owned by DiGard Racing from 1976 through 1980. During that time, he started 151 premier series races, winning 25 of them. Each of those years, he placed in the top five in Cup points, other than 1976 when he took eighth place. His aggressive driving style and outspoken personality earned him the nickname "Jaws," a reference to the 1975 film about a killer shark. That moniker was coined by Hall of Fame driver Cale Yarborough in an interview after Darrell crashed him out of the 1977 Southern 500. Cale later recommended Darrell to succeed him as driver of the Mountain Dew car for Hall of Famer Junior Johnson.

At the height of Darrell's success—12 checkered flags each in the 1981 and 1982 seasons—he was winning about once every three weeks while stacking up back-to-back Cup Series championships. In '81, his 12 wins were part of 21 top fives in 31 races. In '82, Darrell won both NASCAR races on the schedule at four different tracks—Nashville, Bristol, Talladega, and North Wilkesboro—a feat that hasn't been duplicated since. And in 1985, he collected his third championship with three wins and 21 top tens in 28 races.

Darrell drove Tide-sponsored Chevrolets for Rick Hendrick Racing from 1987 through 1990, scoring nine NASCAR Cup Series wins, including the highly coveted Daytona 500 in 1989. All told, from 1975 to 1989, Darrell won at least one race each year. But the 14-year win streak ended in 1990 as he went winless in 23 races. Darrell bounced back with two wins in 1991 and three more in 1992. But over the next eight years, his career went into a tailspin. The last decade of the 20th century was marked by a 251-race winless streak that culminated in Darrell's retirement in 2000. He recalls, "I was one of the best drivers that had ever been in the sport, and all of a sudden I was one of the worst drivers that had ever been in the sport. And that was humiliating."

So how did the three-time Cup champion and winningest NASCAR driver of the 1980s find himself outside victory lane for almost the last decade of his career? Darrell's first couple of seasons as driver/owner of the No. 17 Western Auto car went well, but the next three years proved quite costly. The victories stopped as the company's engine building program lost $1.8 million. Then, just when his team was becoming competitive again in 1995, Darrell broke three ribs in a wreck with Dale Earnhardt Sr. battling for the win on the final lap at the All-Star Race in Charlotte, North Carolina. "That really was the beginning of the end," Darrell says. "I lost my confidence."

Darrell cut his financial losses by selling his team. He then drove competitively for Dale Earnhardt's team, DEI, whenever they needed a replacement driver, before ending his illustrious career with a multicar team sponsored by Kmart. Ironically, the 2012 NASCAR Hall of Fame inductee, who finished in the top 10 in nearly half of his 809 career races, walked away from the sport feeling like a failure. "It was hard to accept that all those years I had won all of those races, and then all of a sudden I couldn't win a race. I'm the world's greatest driver—what do you mean I can't win a race?"

Darrell says his decision to leave Rick Hendrick's team and start his own team in 1991 without first seeking God's direction through prayer proved to be the false start that he regrets most across his Hall of Fame career. "When I started my race team, Stevie asked me, 'Have you prayed about this?' and I said, 'No, I really haven't, but I'm going to.' And then it turned out to be a disaster. I should have asked first and then made a decision based on what the Lord told me, but I didn't."

Darrell and Stevie have witnessed the power of prayer save their marriage. When Darrell was in his early 30s, he knelt in prayer with his pastor, repented of his selfishness, and invited Jesus Christ to be his Savior and Lord. "It was all about me," Darrell confesses. "When you're a driver, you can never admit that you're wrong. You always have to be right, and I had taken that to an extreme."

Though Stevie had been a Christian since before they got married, she hadn't grown in her faith while chasing her husband's obsession with winning on the track. And after 10 years of marriage, her prayers to fall deeper in love with Jesus were being answered as well. "In my misery, I called out for help in seeking the Lord," she says. "My hunger for the Word of God has never been satisfied. It's my favorite subject. It's just what I love occupying my mind with the most." And Darrell's appetite for God's Word also grew as Stevie would read him her weekly Bible study notes while they drove together on weekends to their next speedway venue. Along the way, they also listened to cassette tapes of Bible teaching by Pastor Charles Swindoll and contemporary worship music by Michael Card.

The Waltrips had also been praying for some time that God would give them children. They experienced two miscarriages over a five-year period, and two years later they were still longing for a child of their own. In the midst of their heartache, they sat side by side and prayed, "Dear Lord, if You want us to have a child, then You are able to give us a child. But if You don't, then we'll be satisfied with that answer as well." A few months later, Stevie learned that she was pregnant. After nearly 20 years of marriage, their baby daughter Jessica was born in 1987. A week later, Darrell won his first race of the season. Stevie was 37 at the time, but she still sensed that God wasn't done growing their family. Five years later, Sarah Kaitlyn was born, and Stevie and Darrell, now in their 40s, were parenting another newborn. "We'd been wanting them for so long, and the Lord finally gave us both of them," Stevie recalls as her voice breaks with emotion more than 30 years later.

The Waltrips testify that their faith was forged by learning to trust God in the really hard times and when life doesn't make sense. "Before I got on my knees and asked the Lord to come into my life and turn my life around, before I did that, I won a lot of races," Darrell recalls. "And you would think that when you bent the knee and asked the Lord to come into your life that things would be easier, but they weren't. They were much, much harder. And I never won that many races after that. I think when you put the Lord first in your life, a lot of things change in your marriage and career. And for me those changes were huge because I had never lived in that world before."

Still, Stevie says she wouldn't have it any other way. "We wouldn't want to go through it again, but we wouldn't take anything for it, because we had the Lord and we knew He had a plan. We knew how much He loved us, and we knew it was for our good and His glory."

When Darrell finally decided to exchange the roll cage and a steering wheel for the FOX broadcast booth and a microphone, it seemed like a natural transition for the man who had given such flamboyant and controversial media interviews throughout his racing career. After commentating for FOX on more than 330 races and 1,500 practice and qualifying sessions, Darrell sums up his broadcast career accordingly:

"I won 84 races and three championships, but I never had as much fun as I had as a broadcaster. It was also a great time of growing closer to the Lord. I started listening to the Lord. I would pray first and then make a decision instead of making a decision and then praying about it."

But nothing could have prepared Darrell for his first television broadcast on February 18, 2001, featuring the Daytona 500. It was also the first race that Darrell's brother, Michael, would win after 462 consecutive Cup starts. But all that was overshadowed by the wreck in Turn 4 on the race's final lap that took the life of Dale Earnhardt Sr., the sport's most iconic figure of that era. Darrell recalls the surreal feeling as he witnessed Michael leading the race on the final lap, followed by Dale Earnhardt Jr. in second and Dale Sr. in third. "It was obvious Dale Sr. was driving like he never had driven before. He was blocking. He was trying to keep people from getting to my brother and his son." During one television break, Darrell remembers telling his broadcast partners, Larry McReynolds and Mike Joy, that Dale Sr. was going to get wrecked if he kept trying to block drivers from catching up with Dale Jr. and Michael. And that's exactly what happened as Sterling Marlin hooked Dale Sr.'s bumper, causing him to go headfirst into the wall at 160 miles per hour.

There in the broadcast booth, Darrell suffered a wide swing of emotions, wanting to revel in the biggest moment of his brother's life and at the same time fearing the worst for his longtime competitor and friend who had hired Michael to drive for DEI despite never winning a Cup Series race. When Darrell arrived at Halifax Medical Center, two miles from the world-renowned speedway, he was ushered in to be with the Earnhardt family. Dale Sr.'s wife, Teresa, accompanied him to the hospital room where her husband had already died from his injuries. The emotional trauma left Darrell with no memory of his hospital visit. "I did that, but I don't remember doing it," he explains.

Still in shock, NASCAR raced the following weekend in Rockingham, North Carolina, and Darrell was back in the broadcast booth for his grief-stricken audience. "I was the right guy at the right time," he says. "Dale Sr. and I were friends. I had driven his cars for him. We were buddies and I knew Dale really well." Darrell believes that, for the first time ever, Dale Sr. had been racing for someone other than himself to win. "Dale was all about Dale, and Dale wanted to win, but this day in the Daytona 500, he cared more about Michael and his son finishing first and second on NASCAR's most revered racetrack than anything else."

More than 20 years later, the Waltrips still get emotional when talking about that fateful day. "Superman died that day, and that's how the community looked at him," Stevie says. "It's still hard to believe that it happened. Darrell and I loved him so much." They had gotten to see the driver nicknamed "The Intimidator" in a different light. For years, Stevie had personally greeted Dale Sr. on pit road with an index card bearing a handwritten Bible verse that he excitedly taped inside his car before every race. "I had written Scripture for Darrell and put it in his car, and that always gave me a sense of peace knowing that the power of the Word was in his car." After a while, Dale Sr. asked her, "Where's mine?" Stevie's Bible verse for Dale Sr. on the day of his last race was Proverbs 18:10: "The name of the LORD is a strong tower; the righteous run to it and are safe" (NKJV). "On that particular Sunday, I know that the Lord gave me that Scripture to give to us and Dale's family the assurance that he was with the Lord that day," she says. "It did give a lot of comfort and assurance."

The Bible, the Waltrips say, has been their foundation and anchor through the best and worst of times for more than 40 years. It's their source of godly wisdom, peace, strength, and contentment, which is why they've hosted a Bible study at their home in Franklin, Tennessee, for the past 35 years. And it's why they serve on the board of directors for Motor Racing Outreach, a ministry they helped start in the 1980s to evangelize and disciple the professional racing community.

The Waltrips say their marriage is a picture of the power of the gospel and what can happen when forgiveness is practiced in a relationship. "Jesus made the difference in our tumultuous marriage," Stevie says. "And when you personally receive Jesus's forgiveness, then He can heal any relationship when people are willing to sincerely seek reconciliation. I think some of the most important words in life are saying, 'I'm sorry. I was wrong. Will you forgive me?'"

3

Chase Briscoe

Finding God in the Valley

DECLARING GOD'S GOODNESS and praising Him when times are great seems appropriate, right? But what happens when things aren't going well? On the worst day of your life, is God still worthy of your praise? Could you praise God in the middle of unfathomable loss, pain, or devastation?

If we're honest, probably no one wants to have their faith tested or their love for God measured by their response to suffering. But just like on the racetrack, challenges are ever-present in the race called life. In fact, as you're reading this right now, you'll likely find yourself in one of three lanes: in the middle of a challenge, coming out of a challenge, or about to confront a challenge.

You know when drivers are racing three wide how one ill-timed move can change the fortunes for everyone on the track? Similarly, the way someone responds to a personal crisis or challenge can impact many others—for better or worse.

For Chase Briscoe, former driver of the No. 14 Ford Mustang for Stewart-Haas Racing, his initial response to the hardest day of his life came via the following Instagram post:

5/19/20 will be a day I'll never forget. So much was happening between finding out the gender of our first baby the day before, going back racing finally after the [COVID] virus, and then the worst news I could have heard. I'll never forget the feelings I felt as I FaceTimed my amazing wife during her doctor's visit for "Baby Briscoe" from the infield of Darlington wishing so desperately that I could be by her side to hear the heartbeat for the first time as I sat in the rain. The nurse came in with the doppler machine and they struggled to find anything but reassured us this happens quite often and that they would do an ultrasound so we could see our daughter again at her 12-week mark and see how she was progressing. As I watched the doctor do all the stuff on the ultrasound I'll never forget when she said "Now for the heartbeat" and then the empty black screen I saw and hearing her say "I'm so sorry." It was like time stopped, nothing else even mattered. It was unlike anything I had heard or felt before as I watched my wife's face turn from joy to instant depression. I'll never understand why it happened but I know that God has a plan and even though we don't understand it, He has a reason. Marissa and I will become stronger and will try again but it still doesn't take away the pain now. We greatly appreciate everyone's thoughts and prayers.[1]

When Chase returned home a couple of days before the scheduled race in Darlington, South Carolina, he and Marissa talked and prayed for hours about whether they should share with the public the devastating news about the death of their unborn child. "I knew there was going to be some way that God used it for good," Chase says.

A few days later, when Chase took the lead in the Toyota 200 Xfinity Series race with about 50 laps to go, he started crying as he was overcome with a flood of grief and emotion that he had been suppressing while trying to be strong for his wife. "I remember the last 15 to 20 laps constantly talking to the Lord in prayer, asking Him to just let me use our family tragedy to glorify You, no matter the circumstances."

Then, on the final lap of the race, Chase brushed against the wall as Kyle Busch passed him for the lead. "It's the only time in my life where I've ever hit the wall and somehow gained speed," he says. "I experienced this supernatural feeling inside the car and I beat him back to the finish line."

As soon as Chase climbed out of his vehicle, he dropped to one knee and said a prayer beside his racecar. And when he stood up, he had this to say to the NASCAR reporter as he wiped tears from his eyes: "This is for my wife. And this is the hardest week I've ever had to deal with and God is so good. Even when I took the lead with 50 to go, I was crying inside the racecar. And just emotionally, I wasn't there at all. There's nothing other to say except that God is so glorious. This is more than a race win. This is the biggest day of my life after the toughest day of my life. And then to be able to beat the best there is, is so satisfying."[2]

You might think that growing up in a motor racing family instilled in Chase the drive and tenacity to persevere through the toughest challenges. His grandfather, Richard Briscoe, is a legendary sprint car team owner. And Chase's father, Kevin, raced sprint cars for more than 20 years and won more than 150 feature events while collecting championships across Indiana. But even more than his racing lineage, Chase says he is most grateful for growing up in a Christian home where his family attended a Bible-believing church nearly every Sunday. And his childhood summers always included Vacation Bible School. So, it made sense for him at age 12 to profess his faith in Jesus Christ as his Savior and Lord.

It's Chase's identity in Christ that has helped him navigate the highs and lows in life and in a sport that measures success by numbers like starting positions, miles per hour, pit stop times, and the position a racecar finishes when the checkered flag drops. "You are kind of only as good as your last race, and you're always defined by a number," Chase says. "But I know there's a lot more to my self-worth than the position I finish in a race."

Chase Briscoe's journey to the NASCAR Cup Series began when he was only seven years old. That's when he won his first quarter midget heat race, which he followed by winning the featured event later that same evening. At age 13, Chase broke NASCAR Hall of Famer Jeff Gordon's record as the youngest driver to win a 410 Sprint Car Series race. But by age 19, with finances running low, he applied on a whim to a Facebook ad promoting the PEAK Stock Car Dream Challenge for a chance to join Michael Waltrip Racing as a rookie stock car driver.

In 2013, despite having never driven a stock car on pavement or a car with a manual transmission, Chase was chosen from more than 700 applicants to compete against nine prospects in the three-day event in Charlotte. The competition fielded racecars used in the Richard Petty Driving Experience, and drivers were tested in short-track racing, road-course racing, speedway racing, car control and endurance, and media interviews. Even though Chase finished first in all but one of the on-track competitions, he came in second overall.

The next year, Chase moved to Charlotte from his hometown of Mitchell, Indiana, sleeping on friends' couches and air mattresses while trying to network with motor racing teams in hopes of getting an opportunity to drive in the Automobile Racing Club of America (ARCA), a semiprofessional league of stock car racing. After he volunteered 12-hour days in the garage with Cunningham Motorsports for several months, the team's owner was impressed with Chase's work ethic and invited him to drive in two ARCA races in 2015. He finished 10th in his summer debut followed by a fifth-place finish in the fall.

Later that year, on his drive back home to Indiana, Chase took a 45-minute detour to personally thank the owner of Cunningham Motorsports for giving him the opportunity to drive in the ARCA Series. The team owner rewarded Chase's humble appreciation by hiring him to drive the entire 2016 racing schedule. The transition from racing sprint cars to stock cars proved successful as he won six races and captured the ARCA championship. In 2017, Chase advanced to NASCAR's Truck Series. He was named Rookie of the Year and Most Popular Driver while also qualifying for the playoffs. A couple of years later, he earned Rookie of the Year honors in the Xfinity Series and followed that up by winning nine Xfinity races in 2020.

Stewart-Haas Racing promoted Chase in 2021 to compete in the NASCAR Cup Series, where he won Rookie of the Year honors. That same year, Chase and Marissa were blessed with the birth of their son, Brooks. Chase says, "I never understood God's love for me until I became a parent, and it's crazy to fathom how much He loves each and every person on this planet." The following year, in just his 40th career start in NASCAR's premiere racing division, Chase won his first Cup Series race at Phoenix Raceway and qualified for the playoffs.

In 2025, Chase will drive the No. 19 Bass Pro Shops Toyota Camry XSE in the Cup Series for Joe Gibbs Racing following the closure of SHR at the end of the 2024 season. "From a competition standpoint, JGR is the place to be if you want to go win races week in and week out and to race for the championship every year," Chase says. "I am blessed that Johnny Morris and Bass Pro are on board to help us carry on the legacy of the 19 car. For me personally, being an avid outdoorsman, there's a lot of pride in now being a part of the Bass Pro brand and I'm extremely grateful for this partnership. Getting to meet Johnny, I feel like I share a lot of the same values as him and Coach [Gibbs], and I'm ready to get to work and prove that they have made a great choice putting me in this car."[3]

4

Marcus Smith

Merging the Sacred with the Secular

FOR MARCUS SMITH, serving as president and CEO of Speedway Motorsports, LLC, comes with a lot of responsibility and expectations. While stewarding a family legacy forged by his NASCAR Hall of Fame father, Bruton Smith, whose savvy entrepreneurship and big ideas put stock car racing on the map in the 20th century, Marcus has carved out his own track record of success.

Since filling the driver's seat at SM in 2008, Marcus has extended the company's reach across the country by acquiring racetracks in Delaware, Kentucky, and Tennessee to add to a list of company-owned stock car racing venues in New Hampshire, Georgia, North Carolina, Texas, and California. More recently, SM resurrected North Wilkesboro Speedway in western North Carolina to host the NASCAR All-Star Race in 2023 and 2024. And while Marcus admits that honoring his late father's memory inspires him to never settle for the status quo when it comes to delivering amazing experiences for race fans across the country, he says his primary motivation is biblically driven.

"The Bible tells us to run the race to win. And it's okay to work hard and to want to succeed. I try to do all things as unto Christ. So, to do our very best at something is a biblical principle." Furthermore, Marcus believes that striving to be the best at what you do can't be motivated by selfish ambition or vanity so long as one's aim and priorities are focused on others. Referencing Matthew 22:37–39, he says, "Love is the greatest commandment. Love the Lord your God and love your neighbor as yourself. And I think that loving your coworkers well is important. That makes for a great team."

Marcus still marvels at how his team resurrected North Wilkesboro Speedway, which had hosted its last NASCAR race in 1996 before showcasing the 2023 All-Star Race. "It was a restoration project. It was a rebuilding and renewing project of something that was old. And what people thought was dead is alive again. So, certainly you can draw a lot of inferences from Scripture around that." And the biblical analogies don't stop there for Marcus. "It takes, like the Bible says, all parts of the body are important. Whether it's the head or the ear, the hand, the foot, it takes everything, and that's kind of the way it is for our team. It takes many people and lots of expertise and experience to pull off a project like that. And I was inspired by our team and their excellence and how everything just came together really well. Every challenge was met with good decision-making and challenges were solved. Good attitudes and good teamwork. Great work ethic. All these things combined for a successful project."

Marcus draws timeless insights from the Bible for guidance and wisdom to lead an organization whose 11 racetracks nationwide host nearly a third of NASCAR's Cup Series, Xfinity Series, and Craftsman Truck Series racing schedule each year. And while SM employs about 1,000 full-time employees, the number of seasonal event employees can balloon to 10,000.

Marcus's love for God's Word began as a young child attending Good News Bible Clubs after school. But it was in high school when he realized that having a personal relationship with Jesus Christ gave his life meaning and purpose. As a freshman at the University of North Carolina, his aspirations to become a pediatrician were met with a huge dose of reality when Marcus discovered that calculus, chemistry, and biology classes weren't his formula for success. But he did enjoy serving on campus ministry teams during college. His parents had chosen his middle name, Graham, in honor of evangelist Billy Graham. And during his summer breaks from college while working at the Charlotte Motor Speedway (CMS), painting, landscaping and cleaning up around the track, Marcus was mentored by leaders with Motor Racing Outreach, which has offices at SM's headquarters at CMS.

When Marcus was 20 years old, a conversation he had with Franklin Graham, the late evangelist's eldest son, who was attending the Coca-Cola 600 at CMS, opened his eyes to ministry possibilities he had never considered. Marcus recounts, "Franklin's eyes opened wide and he said, 'Wow, what an opportunity,' and I thought he was talking about the opportunity to host an evangelistic crusade because that's what the Billy Graham's ministry is all about. But he quickly said no, no, not that. He said just being at the speedway provided an opportunity to intersect with so many people and what a great opportunity to make a positive impact on lives, and it kind of flipped a switch in me that your faith in regular life can intersect outside of church and outside of Bible study. That a regular day, it's secular and spiritual all at the same time. And so that was a huge wake-up call to me."

He continues, "And then I kind of realized that we do have this special opportunity to intersect with people in all sorts of ways. In our events there's a nice purpose behind trying to make people happy. Sometimes, we save lives because we've got a lot of paramedics on site and people are in trouble sometimes and we help them out. Other times, we just take an otherwise mundane time and turn it into something really special and really great lifelong memories. We've been able to help create a lot of cool things over the years."

Marcus's father built Charlotte Motor Speedway in 1959, but a few years later he had to file for bankruptcy. Not one to back down from a challenge, the family patriarch reacquired majority control of the racetrack in 1978. By 1992, Speedway Motorsport's trajectory was in full growth mode as CMS became the first modern superspeedway to host night racing. It's not lost on Marcus that his dad's most productive years at SM came later in his career. "He was in his 60s before he really started growing the business. I think about that sometimes and I'm encouraged because I'm in my early 50s. So, I'm just getting started if you look at my dad's track record, and that's why I say you never know what the Lord has in store."

After college, Marcus started his career with SM by selling advertising for the CMS souvenir magazine and sponsorship decals for the racecars competing at the track's 1.5-mile oval.

Over the years, he has steadily climbed the corporate ladder, from manager of new business development (1999) to heading SM's sales and marketing team (2004) to running the Charlotte track and becoming SM president (2008). Along the way he has developed his own penchant for next-level innovation in the world of NASCAR.

In 2011, CMS set a Guinness World Record with the debut of the world's largest HDTV at a sports venue, spanning nearly 16,000 square feet of viewing pleasure for fans. In September 2016, SM converted Bristol Motor Speedway into a college football stadium to host the "Battle at Bristol" between the Tennessee Volunteers and the Virginia Tech Hokies. The game, which Bruton Smith had envisioned 20 years earlier, set an NCAA record with 156,990 people in attendance. And in 2018, CMS reshaped NASCAR history with the innovative ROVAL, a 2.28-mile, 17-turn course that combines the high banks of the traditional oval with a newly designed infield road course.

During a typical race weekend at CMS, fans consume more than 37,000 slices of pizza, 50,000-plus chicken tenders, 5,000-plus gallons of soft drinks, 4,000-plus feet of hot dogs, and more than 165,000 pounds of ice.[1] But to Marcus it means so much more. "It's really about making memories that last a lifetime. And at our events, people gather together from all over the world. And they gather with friends, with family. They give us their time and money and entrust us with these valuable moments in life, and it's our responsibility to be good stewards of that. And to realize that it's far more than just a single day or a weekend or just a ticket. It's really the responsibility of our team to make the best out of these moments that our fans have given us, whether it's NASCAR fans or car show fans, drag racing fans, you name it, we really take that opportunity seriously."

Marcus says his leadership style is guided by four principles: (1) work diligently; (2) pursue excellence; (3) delegate/share responsibilities; and (4) love and respect team members. "My dad always told me to do the right thing. He taught us to inspect what you expect. Exceed expectations. Take care of teammates. Sell to sell again. I really want to do my very best to honor the Lord in everything that we do. And I don't want to get in His way with limiting what might be. So, we'll see what happens. I think God has far more vast and amazing plans than I could ever ask or imagine."

5

Kelley Earnhardt Miller

A Daughter's Longing

AS CO-OWNER AND CEO OF JR MOTORSPORTS, Kelley
Earnhardt Miller's influence on the stock car racing world
is undeniable. The company she co-owns with her brother,
Dale Earnhardt Jr., boasts multiple championships across the
CARS Late Model Stock Car Tour and NASCAR's Whelen
All-American Series, as well as the Xfinity Series, including
past champions Chase Elliott, William Byron, and Tyler Reddick. But if you think that being the daughter of seven-time
NASCAR champion Dale Earnhardt Sr. paved the way for
her ascension in a male-dominated industry, you would be
guilty of a false start. Actually, in many ways, Kelley's impact
on the sport has come in spite of being told by her late father
that stock car racing was a man's domain. She says, "I was

a tomboy as a kid, so I wanted to race. I wanted to hunt. I wanted to ride motorcycles. I wanted to do all these things. And my dad was always like, 'No, no, no, you're a girl and you can't do this, you can't do that. And race shops are for guys.' And so he would never let me be around that kind of stuff."

As much as Kelley longed to put on the racing helmet and slide into the driver's cage, more than anything she simply wanted quality time with her dad, something that was always in short supply throughout her childhood. Her parents divorced when she was two years old. She and her younger brother, Dale Jr., lived with their mom in Virginia until a house fire forced them to move in with their dad and stepmom, Teresa, when Kelley was eight.

"Life as the child of a famous racecar driver was difficult for me," Kelley writes in her memoir. "Dad's streak of success started when I was only eight years old. I was hurting because of what had happened in our family. I missed my mom and endured conflict with my stepmother. Like all children, I wanted a real relationship with my dad. Unfortunately, that type of relationship simply wasn't available. I wanted Dad's attention, not a photo from victory lane. I longed for him to sit down to dinner with us, to pick me up from school, to come to my programs and sports events, to be part of my life. I just wanted him to do what parents do. . . . Dad's success came with prize money but it also came with a price. It cost me the father-daughter relationship that I hungered for. While I'm proud of Dad's accomplishments on the racetrack, they resulted in great personal pain for me."[1]

When Kelley turned 16, her dad gifted her with a nearly new silver 1987 Chevrolet Monte Carlos SS Fastback. The car was impressive, but it made the wrong impression with Kelley.

"He had no idea how much I needed and wanted him to be part of my world," she writes. "I would have given up the SS Fastback in a split second and all the other material goods he provided just to have some quality time with him, just to hear him say he loved me and felt I was important, to have him demonstrate genuine interest in me."

Kelley attended UNC Wilmington from 1990 to 1993 and majored in business management with a concentration in production and inventory. Between attending classes and working part-time at the mall, she rarely made the four-hour drive home. Keeping the pain of her past and the lingering emptiness in her rearview mirror seemingly was best managed by keeping her distance from the source of her neglect.

Then, one day her dad unexpectedly called her on the phone. "My dad really missed me and wanted me to move home," Kelley says. "And, so we made a deal that if I moved home and finished my schooling at UNC Charlotte that he would let me race." Finally, at 21, Kelley began racing street stock cars for six months at a local track in Concord, North Carolina. She then joined her two brothers racing late model stock cars on short tracks throughout the Carolinas, Virginia, and Tennessee, often beating both brothers to the finish line.

Kelley thrived on the adrenaline rush that driving a racecar provided, but more gratifying was the opportunity to spend weekends with her brothers. "The pressures of being a female and racing with older men and things like that were difficult," she says. "But I loved being able to go alongside my brothers. It was a time that we got to spend time together." Yet while she and her brothers competed in nearly 100 races over three years, her dad's busy schedule prevented him from attending any of his children's races. "I think he just wanted me to go to college," Kelley says about her dad, who had dropped out of school in the eighth grade. "He saw bigger things for me and how tough it would be to be a female in the NASCAR world." So, after graduating from college in 1995, Kelley went to work at Action Performance, the souvenir sales company that became the benchmark in NASCAR merchandising. Her many roles during a six-year span there included vice president of sales and vice president of procurement. Meanwhile, her brothers continued pursuing racing alongside their father. Over the next several years, Dale Sr. continued his dominance on the NASCAR circuit while Dale Jr. won back-to-back Xfinity championships before joining the Cup Series.

Then February 18, 2001, happened. And everything changed forever.

In just his second career start, Dale Jr. finished second for his father's Cup team at the Daytona 500. Trailing in third place on the final lap, Dale Sr.'s car, the jet-black No. 3 Chevrolet, slammed head-on into the wall at Turn 4. The elder Earnhardt was killed instantly. Kelley witnessed the tragedy on television while caring for her five-month-old daughter at her grandmother's house. It had been about three weeks since she last spoke to her dad. "At the time, our relationship was really shaky and rocky," she says. "One of the things that my dad always said was that 'if something happens to me in the racecar, I was doing what I love.' And so, my peace with that accident kind of came through that statement."

About six months later, Kelley stepped away from her executive sales position with the souvenir merchandising company to become Dale Jr.'s agent and business manager with JR Motorsports. It seemed only natural that the two siblings unite in business. They were always there for each other growing up, like the time Kelley voluntarily withdrew from the high school she attended in ninth grade to enroll at the military boarding school where Dale Jr. had been sent after being expelled from a private Christian school for repeatedly clowning around in class. Now it was time for Kelley to once again look out for her younger brother's best interest, especially as his career and popularity began to soar in the Cup Series.

With Kelley's heavy workload at JRM, she and her husband entrusted the care of their young daughter to a nanny during the weekdays. Not only did their nanny provide a nurturing environment for their daughter, she also helped Kelley grow in her relationship with Christ. "As she came into our house, I started really learning about the connection to Jesus, and not just, you know, you're a Christian, you believe in God and you go to church," Kelley says. "Everything was centered around Christ for her. So, that's really when I started pursuing a real Christ-focused life, when I was almost 30. It's something I still work on every day, because it's just hard for me. My personality is controlling. My personality is that I'll figure out how to get something done. I don't have patience, don't like to wait. I am probably most like my dad in terms of personality and common sense and a go-getter." Her favorite Bible verse is Jeremiah 29:11: "'For I know the plans I have for you,' declares the LORD, 'plans to prosper you and not to harm you, plans to give you hope and a future'" (NIV).

JRM has grown exponentially under Kelley's leadership. The company employs about 130 people and fields four teams in the Xfinity Series. The once aspiring racecar driver who longed for the opportunity to prove that she could compete on the same track with her brothers now thrives on helping other fledgling drivers chase their dreams of competing in

NASCAR. Over the past two decades, Kelley has received numerous industry awards and accolades for her achievements while leading JRM to unprecedented growth. And as a mother, Kelley has supported her two daughters and son in their dirt track racing pursuits. She says, "The biggest reason I do this is for all the families we employ. I try to remember for myself daily to be the hands and feet of Jesus. I want somebody to look at me and tell that I'm Christ-centered in whatever I do during the day. Just trying to keep that front and center in a world that's broken and fallen."

6

Dave Alpern

How to Become Irreplaceable

IN 2016, Dave Alpern was named president of Joe Gibbs Racing. But he wasn't happy about the promotion.

During his more than two decades with the company, Dave had done nearly every job in the corporate office. Beginning as an unpaid intern just out of college, he worked out of a broom closet with no electrical outlets. From gofer to indispensable brain trust, his career blossomed with JGR from its start-up days with a handful of employees to more than 500 on the payroll today. Joe Gibbs affectionately called Dave the "T-shirt guy" for creating and launching the company's merchandising and souvenir line in the early 1990s, and the entry-level title followed Dave for years, even as Gibbs sought his counsel alongside his executive team before making strategic boardroom decisions. Prior to being named JGR's president, Dave led the company's consumer products, communications, and sponsorship divisions. His executive leadership roles had him working with corporate-level executives from companies such as Toyota, FedEx, Mars, Stanley, Coca-Cola, and Comcast. He had been invited to the White House five times in recognition of JGR's NASCAR Cup Series championships in 2000, 2002, 2005, 2015, and 2019.

So why was Dave less than enthusiastic about becoming president of the winningest team in NASCAR history? It wasn't for lack of ambition or fear of taking on a new challenge. Dave had overcome a lot growing up in northern Virginia. In sixth grade, he was diagnosed with Tourette's syndrome, a nervous system disorder that causes involuntary twitching, blinking, and grunting, among other symptoms. The chronic condition worsened throughout his teenage years. During the first week of his freshman year in high school, a bully stuffed Dave's 5-foot, 85-pound body in a trash can to the amusement of his peers. After high school, when Dave was not accepted into any of his top three college choices, he commuted locally to George Mason University. But those college rejections were blessings in disguise as he met his future wife, Stacey, at GMU while earning a communications degree.

By early adulthood, Dave's Tourette's was less noticeable outwardly. And by his late 30s, his teenage prayers of not wanting to be noticed had done a 180-degree turn for the beloved husband and father of three sons. Dave says, "There are many entries in my prayer journal where I was wrestling with God, 'I know You made me to be more than the T-shirt guy.'" For years, he was frustrated that his corporate profile within the company didn't thoroughly reflect his contributions in executive-level meetings. "I would think to myself, 'Is really all I am is the T-shirt guy?' because behind the scenes, because of my relationship with the Gibbs [family], they would pull me into everything. Like we'd have huge meetings on a driver crisis or whatever, and I'd be in them. I loved that they would seek my counsel. And I would always have a seat at the table to offer wisdom or whatever. But when we would leave that room, no one outside that room knew that I had anything to do with it. And so it wasn't anything they were doing wrong. It was just me and my ego."

Despite Dave's longing for more responsibility within the company, he never imagined being president of JGR. Coach Gibbs's eldest son, J.D., had proven quite capable of leading the family-owned business in that role. J.D. was revered throughout the company, the NASCAR industry, and corporate sponsors alike for his humble and personable servant leadership style. In fact, J.D. had been Dave's best friend since middle school. "I would say J.D. was a key catalyst for me professing my faith in Christ," he says. The Gibbs family hosted weekly Young Life student Bible study meetings at their home, and as the ever-popular high school quarterback, J.D. could draw a crowd. After being dismissive of the gospel for several years, Dave could no longer deny that Jesus Christ died on a cross for the forgiveness of his sins and that God raised His Son from death to life so he too could inherit eternal life in heaven. Halfway through his senior year of high school, Dave finally reasoned that if Jesus hadn't been crucified and resurrected, His disciples would not have become martyrs for a lie or hoax.

Throughout their college years, Dave and J.D. reconnected with their 12-member Young Life Bible study group during summer and holiday breaks. Still to this day, Dave maintains a text group chat with those same high school friends called Band of Brothers, and they get together often. He says, "And so I had this experience where J.D. was kind of the ringleader, and all of those guys would point to him as one of the key instruments of them coming to faith in Christ. And then throughout our lives, J.D. continued to be what I always called my spiritual compass. Like for being a Christian in business, being a Christian husband, being a Christian father, I would just kind of watch J.D. He was the guy that I just looked at as an example for all of those things."

When J.D. invited Dave to help him and his father start their fledgling stock car racing enterprise in the early 1990s, his struggling self-confidence was energized. "J.D. could have picked anybody. J.D. had a lot of friends. And I remember asking him later in life, 'Why did you ask me?' And he said, 'Because I knew we could count on you,' because of some of my traits he had seen through high school, this loyalty, the dependability, toughness. The fact that J.D. picked me was a boost of confidence for me, and then it became evident that I didn't want to let them down."

Dave says his inspiration for screenprinting Joe Gibbs Racing on T-shirts and hats was motivated by a desire to make himself indispensable to the company's success. "I wanted to be around because I wanted to grow, and yes, I think this race team's going be successful because of these guys, but I wanted my faith to grow and I wanted to be around these guys and learn from them." The T-shirts and hats would sell out quickly at RFK Stadium, home of the Washington Redskins, where Coach Gibbs held legendary status from his Super Bowl victories in the 1980s and early 1990s. "It became a very lucrative business for Joe Gibbs Racing," Dave says. "And I kind of just got in at the right time and learned how to do it. I was creating my own niche within the company. That created the value for them to hire me full-time. And I learned how product licensing worked and that became my thing. I was a consumer products guy, but no one asked me to do that. I just did it and J.D. encouraged me."

Then, 25 years later, Coach Gibbs and J.D. asked Dave to do the unimaginable and succeed J.D. as president of JGR. At the time, J.D. was in the middle of a five-year battle with the neurological disease that would take his life in 2019. "And it wasn't until really 20-plus years into my career, when J.D. got sick, that the light bulb went off that God was preparing me for a job that I never contemplated ever," Dave says. "I had gone to work for Joe Gibbs Racing and there are two sons. I'm never going to be the president, nor do I want to be, but I was sort of at this spot where there's not really anywhere else to go inside this company. And in the back of my mind, I always thought that it was in the cards for me that I would go use this amazing experience and go do something else. And then J.D. got sick, and it was kind of like, okay, now I understand why I had to do all those other things. I had to understand all of the details in the minutiae to be prepared to do this job. I can tell you, within a week of being the president, I would have given anything to be the T-shirt guy again. And I wanted my friend back. I wanted J.D. to be healthy."

Among the many lessons that Dave has learned during his career with JGR, he says that one of the most profound is this: "The who is more important than the what. What I mean by that in business is who you're doing it for is more important than what you're doing. And we could have been selling coat hangers at JGR and it wouldn't have mattered. We were praying every Monday morning for all the employees by name. I was in this culture with these people, these spiritual giants that I admired. And so I really wanted to stick around."

Dave says that when God doesn't answer his prayers the way he would like, he trusts the Scriptures that say His ways are better than our ways and His thoughts are higher than our thoughts. "I have 35 years of seeing God's faithfulness, and that outweighs any doubts that I have." So, when Dave's prayers for healing from Tourette's never came to pass, he didn't stop praying. "Many of my early prayers were centered around 'God take this from me.' I didn't understand why isn't He taking this away from me. But it also was the thing that drew me to Him, because obviously when you have a thorn, it causes you to fall to your knees. And when I talk to folks who have some sort of a thorn, I always tell them that the thorn is a blessing in many ways because it is going to drive you to your knees. And God doesn't always choose to take it away." That's why one of Dave's favorite Bible verses is Romans 15:13: "May the God of hope fill you with all joy and peace as you trust in him, so that you may overflow with hope by the power of the Holy Spirit" (NIV).

Dave now describes living with Tourette's as more of an internal struggle with obsessive-compulsive tendencies, as his outward symptoms have waned considerably. He says one blessing of his condition is that it revealed the best qualities in his wife-to-be when they were dating in college. "I was so self-conscious about it, and worried what people would think because I would twitch or I would grunt or I would whatever. And it was a nonfactor to Stacey at the time. She was the most Christlike person I'd ever met and had a deep faith that was demonstrated through the way she handled that with me."

When Dave speaks to university students in business schools across the country about the most important leadership qualities, he offers a unique perspective. "I always say character and authenticity, which are two that people rarely think of. Our mission at JGR is to go fast. We say that about everything. Does this make us go fast? But we have plenty of people to do that. If we go fast but we lose sight of treating people the right way and honoring God, then I've not done my job. And so that's the burden that I have. And that was directly from J.D., I believe."

7

Aric Almirola

Why Baptism Matters

CLIMBING OUT OF THE NO. 10 Smithfield Ford for Stewart-Haas Racing after the final race of 2023, Aric Almirola was brimming with joy. But it wasn't because he was in victory lane. He actually had placed 13th at Phoenix Raceway on that first Sunday in November. Two weeks earlier he had a top-10 finish at Homestead-Miami Speedway, followed by a second-place finish at Martinsville Speedway in Virginia. Not a bad way to close out a 16-year run of chasing checkered flags in the NASCAR Cup Series for some of NASCAR's most iconic teams owned by legends such as Richard Petty, Joe Gibbs, Dale Earnhardt Jr., and Tony Stewart.

Then, in mid-December 2023, Aric announced on social media that he would be coming out of retirement to drive part-time in the 2024 Xfinity Series for Joe Gibbs Racing. "Twenty years ago, I got a phone call from Coach and J.D. Gibbs that changed my life. I'm so grateful and humbled that Coach called and asked me to come back home to JGR and finish my career here."[1] It seemed Aric's career had come full circle, like a race that ends where it starts. His breakthrough opportunity to fulfill his childhood dream of becoming a professional racecar driver had started with a prayer—a long prayer that he now acknowledges was pretty self-centered. But God answered Aric's prayer even though he truly didn't know the ramifications of what he was requesting.

In the fall of 2003, Aric's life took an unexpected turn while he was pursuing a mechanical engineering degree in college. A program that had been launched by JGR and the late NFL Hall of Fame defensive end Reggie White to help minorities with the desire and talent to pursue a career in motorsports opened the door for Aric to chase his dream. He auditioned to be selected for the program by showcasing his skills at a driver combine at Hickory Motor Speedway in North Carolina. After the tryout, Aric drove back home to Florida without turning on his vehicle's radio even once. "I remember praying the same prayer over and over and over for eight hours," he recalls. "I kept asking God to please allow me to have this only if He wants it for me. And that if this is not what He wants for me, don't let me get this opportunity only to fail. I wanted assurance from God that if this was an opportunity, that it was an opportunity from Him, and that it was going to be an opportunity that I was going to be able to succeed at." At the time, Aric admits, his relationship with God was mostly one-sided. He would call on God when he needed something, but otherwise Aric preferred to be in the driver's seat of his life. So when he received an invitation from JGR to drive for the team in NASCAR's developmental Late Model Series, Aric was full speed ahead.

A Tampa native of Cuban descent, Aric had started racing go-karts when he was eight years old. At 14, he finished fourth in the 1998 season-ending standings for the World Karting Association. In 2000, he advanced to driving open-wheel modifieds—2,750-pound racecars that put out more than 700 horsepower. That same year, he won the Rookie of the Year title in two separate modified divisions. Two years later, Aric graduated from open-wheel Modifieds to the Sunbelt Super Late Model Division, where he finished runner-up in the Rookie of the Year standings. In 2005–2006, he raced in the Truck and Xfinity Series before making his first career start in the Cup Series at Las Vegas Motor Speedway on March 11, 2007, just three days before his 23rd birthday. Over the next four years, Aric competed in the Truck, Xfinity, and Cup Series with JGR and Dale Earnhardt, Inc., as opportunities increasingly came his way.

The 2012 season had Aric slated to drive full-time for JR Motorsports in the Xfinity Series, but then a phone call from Richard Petty, the "King of NASCAR" and all-time winningest driver, changed everything when he anointed Aric to drive his No. 43 Ford. The 2014 season proved to be his breakthrough year when he won his first career Cup Series race on July 6 at Daytona International Speedway. During his six seasons piloting the iconic No. 43 Ford for Richard Petty Motorsports, Aric not only scored the organization's first Cup Series victory since 1999, he also won a pole for the fastest qualifying lap and earned 11 top fives and 31 top tens.

Then, in 2017, Aric was involved in a violent, multicar accident at nearly 190 miles per hour at Kansas Speedway. Rescue workers had to cut off the top of the racecar to extract Aric from the car as he writhed in pain. X-rays revealed that he suffered a compression fracture to his T5 vertebra. The wreck triggered a new NASCAR safety protocol requiring postrace height inspections of the racecar to prevent similar injuries. "I was panicked. I was worried. I was just really hoping that I was not going to be paralyzed." Aric was sidelined for seven races. His rehabilitation included swimming and weight lifting, and he returned stronger than ever, earning three top-10s to complete the season.

Aric's return from a back-breaking accident on the racetrack garnered him a contract with Stewart-Haas Racing in 2018. Co-owner Tony Stewart, a member of the NASCAR Hall of Fame, welcomed the opportunity to again join forces with his former JGR teammate. In his first race with SHR, Aric drove from his 37th starting position to lead the Daytona 500 with half a lap to go before contact with another car sent him into the wall and an 11th place finish. Aric made the NASCAR Playoffs four consecutive years with SHR (2018–2021). In fact, in his first year with the organization, he finished a career-best fifth place in the championship standings. His six top fives, 18 top tens, and 305 laps led in 2020 were all season bests. His third-place finish at Talladega tied him with Dale Earnhardt Jr. for eight consecutive top-ten finishes at the Alabama superspeedway, earning him the nickname Speedway Ace.

Looking back on his racing career, Aric says that God has been faithful even when he wasn't. He says that until 2016, he would attend prerace chapel services more out of superstition than to truly worship God. "I thought that chapel service was like a lucky rabbit's foot, and when I would go, I would hope that it would bring me good luck. And then on weekends where it didn't bring me good luck and I would have a bad race, I wouldn't go to the chapel service the next week. I didn't understand what was going on. I was making more money than I'd ever made in my life. I was a NASCAR Cup Series driver full-time. I had a beautiful family, everybody's healthy. And yet, I felt some sort of emptiness and some sort of void and I couldn't explain it."

When Aric asked his wife, Janice, what she thought could be the issue, she asked him where God was in his equation for success. That's when Aric reached out to a Motor Racing Outreach chaplain and prayerfully repented of taking Jesus's seat on the throne of his life. "I had finally come to a conclusion that I cared more about my relationship with Christ than results on the track. What I cared about was having a fulfillment that only a relationship with Christ could fulfill. And that really changed everything for me." Ironically, that's also when Aric began experiencing the most success on the racetrack.

In more than 450 career Cup Series starts, he has earned three wins, 30 top fives, 96 top tens, and six poles, and he has led 1,147 laps. He also has five Xfinity Series victories and two Craftsman Truck Series wins. But for all his great memories on the racetrack, Aric says a day away from the track in October 2019 tops them all: the day of his baptism. He even posted a video of it on Instagram to share with the world, along with the words of Romans 10:9–10: "If you openly declare that Jesus is Lord and believe in your heart that God raised him from the dead, you will be saved. For it is by believing in your heart that you are made right with God, and it is by openly declaring your faith that you are saved" (NLT). Here's an excerpt from Aric's narration of the video:

October 24, 2019, a day I'll never forget.

I finally got baptized. Let me start by saying this is not about me at all. By no means am I doing this to bring attention to myself. This is purely to bring honor and glory to God. I have accepted Jesus Christ as my Savior in my heart and I am publicly confessing, like the Bible says to do. It seems so crazy and simple that this is all I have to do to have an eternal relationship with my Creator. That for most of my life I had wrestled with it, well not anymore. Today, I accept the grace of God and I commit my life to Christ going forward. . . .

I've always considered myself a Christian, but it wasn't until recently that I started actively pursuing being a Christian day in and day out. This has drastically transformed my life and led me to the point of getting baptized. Baptism is symbolic of a transformation, dying to your old self and old ways, being buried or submerged, and resurrected a new person with a new life to live for Christ. Now this doesn't mean that from this day forward I'm going to be perfect. I'm human. I will continue to fall short in so many ways, but by the grace of God, I know that I now will live an eternity with Him.[2]

Aric says that posting the video of his baptism wasn't his idea. "I kept having this tug on my heart of having it videoed and putting it out there publicly. I guess it was the Holy Spirit whispering to me, just saying that by you doing this and you stepping out in faith and you putting this out there publicly, that even if you impact one person with this video, it's worth it regardless of what criticism you may or may not receive. Now, that was what I was worried about. I was worried about the criticism, and worried about what people would think or what they would say. And I kept getting this whisper that said, 'Don't worry about what anybody else thinks. Don't worry about what anyone else is gonna say. I want you to do this for Me. It's not about you.'"

When Aric first posted his retirement announcement on social media in October 2023, he quoted Proverbs 19:21: "Many are the plans in a person's heart, but it is the LORD's purpose that prevails" (NIV). So when he returned to racing only part-time in the 2024 Xfinity Series, he did so with a specific set of goals. "I want to be involved with helping people," he says. "I have a burning desire to make an impact in other people's lives. I've done an incredible job of worrying about me and me only. Because to be a professional athlete, you have to be extremely selfish. You focus on your needs, yourself. What do you do to make sure you're in shape? What do you do to make sure you're the best racecar driver you can be? What do you do to make the most money you can make? Like, all of those things are completely self-centered. And I am at a point in my life to where I'm ready to turn the page on having all the focus on me, and I'm ready to focus on helping other people."

8

Jimmy Makar

Trusting God's Plan

HOW DO YOU CONVINCE a NASCAR crew chief to leave a legendary race team and its Cup Series champion driver to join a start-up competitor with zero experience in the sport? Tell him that people are more important than parts on a racecar.

Jimmy Makar says that refreshing business philosophy resonated with him like an engine firing on all cylinders, especially in the world of stock car racing where mechanics and pit crews can sometimes be thought of as a dime a dozen. Why would you leave Roger Penske to go to a fledgling team owned by an NFL football coach? Jimmy understood the sentiment. And logically, he agreed that the career move was high-risk, maybe even a little reckless. "There was just something about it that was intriguing," Jimmy says when asked about the offer from Super Bowl champion head coach Joe Gibbs in 1991 to join him in launching a NASCAR team from nothing. "His idea of team building and people, and listening to Joe's priorities—God, family, job—that resonated with me a lot."

Jimmy had moved from New Jersey to Charlotte in 1976, towing along his father's wrecked Cup Series car to seek assistance from legendary mechanics Banjo Matthews and Robert Gee. The Makar family didn't race, but the NASCAR enthusiasts did field midpack rides for a few struggling drivers in 1977 and 1978. Jimmy's "repair visit" opened the door to a full-time job with Gee. Over the next 13 years, he worked with Harry Hyde, Ron Benfield, Buddy Parrott, and NASCAR Hall of Fame driver and car owner Junior Johnson. After six years with Blue Max Racing, which won the 1989 Sprint Cup Series championship with Rusty Wallace behind the wheel, Jimmy became Wallace's crew chief when they both moved to Penske South in 1990.

Jimmy left Penske in the middle of the 1991 season after Rusty had won both races at Pocono. The opportunity to crew chief for driver Dale Jarrett, his brother-in-law who was on the rise in the NASCAR circuit, made the opportunity to join Joe Gibbs Racing even more appealing. Jarrett was doing well in Cup with Wood Brothers Racing, having gotten his first career victory in Michigan in 1991. And with the Daytona 500 barely six months away, Jimmy had a tall task in front of him to be ready for green flag racing at Daytona International Speedway.

Meanwhile, Joe Gibbs was leading his Washington Redskins football team to their third championship in 10 seasons. The ultimate multitasker, Coach Gibbs invited Jimmy to be his guest for Super Bowl 26 in Minneapolis on January 26, 1992, just three weeks before JGR's Cup Series debut in the Great American Race at the birthplace of NASCAR. The evening before the Redskins and Buffalo Bills were scheduled to play for the championship, Jimmy and Dale and their spouses attended the Redskins team chapel service with Coach Gibbs. At the conclusion of his message, the chapel speaker asked those who would like to receive God's gift of forgiveness and promise of eternal life to please stand up. Jimmy began to sweat and feel nervous before finally standing up after the speaker repeated himself for the fourth time. Funny thing about it, Jimmy says, is that he later learned from another person in attendance that the speaker had in fact given the invitation just once, not four times like Jimmy had thought. "The Holy Spirit was working in my life, no doubt about it. The Holy Spirit was convicting me to accept Christ. Even when you're not really necessarily looking for Him, He is looking for you."

When Jimmy started with JGR in August 1991, there wasn't even an office or building or mechanic's garage to begin constructing a racecar or team out of. All they had at the very beginning was Interstate Batteries as a primary sponsor and a commitment from Dale Jarrett to drive the No. 18 Chevrolet. Rick Hendrick Motorsports had agreed to supply the engines for JGR. They also sold Joe some old racecars and scrap parts that were left over from the No. 17 Tide car that Darrell Waltrip had driven before leaving Hendrick Motorsports in 1990 to form his own race team. So now Jimmy had engines, a few used racecars, and a mix-and-match inventory of parts and pieces, but still nowhere to put everything. That's when he found a warehouse with a few offices off Harris Boulevard in Charlotte, which he converted into a race shop with a fabrication department, car paint department, and paint booth. And while the race shop was being built out, Jimmy worked from home ordering the remaining parts he needed to assemble the racecars. On the weekends, he would attend the NASCAR races to scout his brother-in-law and try to persuade pit crew members from competing teams to join JGR's start-up operation. Somehow, he sold about 15 people on rolling the dice on a race team's unproven track record.

A wreck knocked Jarrett out of his JGR debut, placing him 36th in the Daytona 500 after starting the race in 35th position. Jarrett went on to finish 19th in the Cup points standings during the team's 1992 inaugural season by securing two top fives and eight top tens. During JGR's second year of existence, Jarrett catapulted to a fourth-place finish in the Cup points standings, with one win, 13 top fives, and 18 top tens. Jimmy won two races over three seasons for JGR with Dale Jarrett driving. But by the end of the 1994 season, Jarrett would move on to drive for Robert Yates Racing. Bobby Labonte succeeded Jarrett behind the wheel at JGR and won 19 races from 1995 through 2000 with Jimmy as his crew chief.

In 2001, Jimmy was named JGR's director of competition, leading the organization's expansion to field multiple Cup, Xfinity, and Truck Series teams. Under his leadership, JGR won five Cup Series championships (2000, 2002, 2005, 2015, 2019) and three Xfinity Series championships (2009, 2016, 2022). By the time JGR won their fifth Cup Series championship in 2019 with Kyle Busch in the driver's seat, Jimmy was serving as senior vice president of racing development and operations. Everything JGR fielded in NASCAR and ARCA was his responsibility. He also assisted in engineering and had a voice in the aerodynamic development of JGR cars. That same 2019 season, JGR had two other teams in the Cup Series championship playoffs with drivers Martin Truex Jr. and Denny Hamlin—the first time a NASCAR team fielded three of the final four contenders. To put an exclamation point on JGR's 2019 season of total dominance, three of their drivers—Kyle Busch, Martin Truex Jr., and Erik Jones—finished first, second, and third in the season finale at Homestead-Miami Speedway. And when the smoke finally settled on the 2022 season, JGR's four Cup Series cars had totaled 19 victories out of 36 races—the most for any team in NASCAR's modern era.

During his 30-plus years with JGR, Jimmy not only witnessed exponential growth in the company and success on the track, but he also grew spiritually. He recalls, "One of the first things Joe did was have a Bible study and have a chaplain come on board. We still to this day start every Monday morning praying over concerns around the shop and families and sponsors and lifting the week up to God. That's a big, big part of getting through tough times that we have certainly experienced over the course of 30-something years of racing. And there's no better example of that than Joe losing two sons and having faith that God is in control and God's got a plan."

For Jimmy, growing in his identity in Christ took years of learning from repeated mistakes, like how to overcome an anger problem that had earned him the nickname "Mad Dog" in the racing shop and on pit road. "It took awhile to be able to accept things and not be angry about it. It's not something that I'm proud of, but it is a part of my walk. And what I've learned to do is go back and apologize and ask forgiveness for screwing up like that. And that was hard to do in the beginning, but for me it's a way for me to move on and be less of a mad dog when things don't go right."

Over time, employees in the company began asking questions about Jimmy's noticeable change in demeanor. A metal fabricator was so intrigued by Jimmy's transformation that he became a Christian when the company chaplain explained how Jimmy's relationship with Christ had given him victory over his once uncontrollable anger. "That's a good example of walking your faith every day and people seeing a change and how that can affect other people," Jimmy says. "Ministry opportunities happen every single day, not just on a mission trip or going to church. It's your daily walk that people watch and get a picture of who you are and what you believe." Kind of like the influence that Joe Gibbs has had on those who work for JGR. "Just because you have faith and trust in God, it doesn't mean that you're going to be successful," Jimmy adds. "The Bible actually tells you that you are going to have trouble as a Christian in this world (John 16:33). But it also tells us to keep faith and trust. And that is one of the things that has been consistent since the beginning of the race team, of not only Joe's faith but many others on the race team."

Off the track, God has given Jimmy a love for those who are quite different from him. Since 2006, he has served a two-week mission in London nearly every summer. "I fell in love with the people over there from the Middle East," he says. "We've seen many people come to Christ. I think that is a place where God is at work with people disenchanted with Islam." Working at JGR for more than three decades has instilled in him a burden for people around the world to personally know that God created them and loves them so much that He allowed His Son to die in their place so their sins could be forgiven and they could live with Him for eternity in heaven. "The gospel is intertwined with everyday life here. Team meetings end with prayer, races start with prayer, our chaplain speaks to everyone on a daily basis. If you haven't seen or heard the gospel at Joe Gibbs Racing, then you got your eyes and ears closed."

Jimmy identifies Philippians 4:12–13 as his life's mission: "I know how to be abased, and I know how to abound. Everywhere and in all things I have learned both to be full and to be hungry, both to abound and to suffer need. I can do all things through Christ who strengthens me" (NKJV). "Life is not going to be easy, and your job is not going to be easy," Jimmy says. "We've been successful because we have stayed true and faithful to doing our job and doing the things that God has called us to do, and I think God honors that in due time. He gives and He takes away. It's His plan. When you realize that's the way things are, it's easier to take tough times. It's still not easy but it's easier. And God's plan is the best plan."

9

Larry McReynolds

Living in Light of Eternity

FOR MORE THAN 20 YEARS, Larry McReynolds has been beloved by NASCAR fans as "America's Crew Chief." Since 2001, he has provided television viewers an insider's look into race teams' strategies for finishing strong. Having won 23 races over 17 years with six different drivers, Larry knows what it takes to roll into victory lane. His 21 poles, 122 top fives, and 209 top tens speak for themselves. But Larry's journey from working full-time at an auto salvage yard to being the crew chief for two Hall of Fame drivers is a story of determined dedication that has taken the Birmingham, Alabama native to the highest of highs and the lowest of lows.

It all started with Larry attending local short-track races with his aunt and grandfather when he was in elementary school. At 13, Larry attended his first NASCAR race and was amazed more by what he saw off the track. "I had finally talked my dad into taking me to Talladega to watch the race," he recalls. "Don't get me wrong, the racing was fascinating. But what fascinated me the most was watching those guys on pit road. Watching Leonard Wood change a front tire and watching Harry Hyde change a front tire. Watching Junior Johnson jack that number 11 car and sling that jack around, that's what fascinated me."

In high school, Larry helped that same aunt and her husband, who was an auto dealership mechanic, transform a street car into a racecar in their basement for her to compete at the local short track. "Take the seats and windows out, put a racing seat in with a roll bar behind it and put the fuel tank up in the trunk, put a number on it, and you got a racecar," Larry says. "I didn't know a three-quarter wrench from a three-quarter bolt, but I was like a sponge and listened and learned everything I could. I guess you could say my racing career started in the basement of their house."

A year later, Larry started working at an auto salvage yard where he continued full-time after graduating from high school. His boss invited him to volunteer as an apprentice mechanic with their late model race team that competed at tracks across the Southeast on the weekends. "I was working every night on that racecar, a lot of times all night. Just in time enough to go home and clean up and go back to the junkyard. We were racing pretty much March to early December, almost every weekend. I didn't really have much of a life. But I knew working on racecars is what I wanted to do. That's what I wanted to do to make a living."

Then Larry's life took an unexpected turn in the summer of 1980. By then he had advanced from salvaging parts from the castaway vehicles dumped on the lot to selling the reclaimed parts from inside the business. One day, when a customer called needing a used auto part, Larry put the caller on hold and ran out the back door of the building to check inventory in the yard. Meanwhile, another employee had failed to lower the forklift parked just outside the back door, and in his haste to serve the customer, Larry ran into the raised forklift and suffered a concussion. While recovering at home for a couple of weeks, he responded to a classified ad in a NASCAR newsletter for a start-up race team in Greenville, South Carolina, needing mechanics and fabricators. A few weeks after his phone interview, the new race team invited Larry to work in the garage as a stock car mechanic on a trial basis for a couple months. About a month into his tryout, he was offered a full-time job. So, at age 21, Larry hooked a U-Haul trailer to his green 1971 Pinto and moved to South Carolina. He says, "My mom and dad both told me, 'You'll be back in six months. You'll be broke. You'll be hungry. We'll feed you, but we're not going to bail you out of debt.' And I told them both, 'As much as I respect what y'all tell me, and you're probably right, but I got to go try this.' And 40-plus years later, I'm still here."

Larry never had an inkling of desire to drive a racecar, but he always wanted to work on a top NASCAR Cup Series car. While he chased that dream in the early 1980s, Larry admits that he got his priorities out of order. He had made a profession of faith in Christ and was baptized in the Church of Christ when he was 12 years old. "We had some family in from out of town, and I made the decision that this was the day I wanted to truly accept Christ and go forward during the closing hymn and be baptized," he recalls. But 10 years later, Larry was in a much different place. "There's no doubt

I had totally drifted away from going to church, still believed in God, still believed in Christ and never lost that, but just was not practicing it whatsoever." When Larry married his wife, Linda, in 1983, he began attending church with her. "As our marriage journey started, I could see that Linda was a pretty devoted Catholic, so I started going to the Catholic church with her. And the more I would go to church with Linda, I started enjoying the Catholic faith." Larry's parents had divorced when he was seven years old, and one of their disagreements was over their church affiliation. "I never went to church with my mom and dad together," he says. "And I did not want any of our kids to experience that. I wanted us to worship God and go to church together as a family." So, in the mid-80s, Larry joined the Catholic church where he and Linda and their three children attended regularly.

In 1988, Larry won his first NASCAR race as a crew chief, with Ricky Rudd behind the wheel of the Quaker State car at Watkins Glen International in New York. A year later, he won another road course with Rudd at Sonoma Raceway north of San Francisco before winning his first oval track race at North Wilkesboro Speedway in North Carolina with driver Brett Bodine. Larry's career as a crew chief found another gear in 1991 when he joined Robert Yates Racing to team up with driver Davey Allison. "For the first time I felt like not only do I have all the resources to win races, we got all the resources to go out and compete for a championship." And compete they did. Davey Allison made Larry an 11-time winning crew chief over the course of two-and-a-half years—winning five races and the All-Star Race in '91, followed by five more victories in '92, including the prestigious Daytona 500 and a second consecutive All-Star Race. "The sky was the limit," Larry says.

When Davey took the checkered flag at Talladega Super-speedway in 1992, Larry became the winning crew chief at the same track where he'd attended his first NASCAR race with his father 20 years earlier. "Dreams come true," Larry says. "Whether you believe it or not, they do come true." But Larry's dream turned into a nightmare about 14 months later when Davey was killed in a helicopter crash at Talladega. He recalls, "When [Davey] got killed July 13, 1993, there's probably nobody I ever knew who had their priorities more in order. His priorities as a racecar driver. His priorities as a dad, his priorities as a husband and son. But more than anything, his belief in God. My relationship with Davey as a driver/crew chief was just miniscule. We were best friends. I didn't know if I wanted to move on with racing. I had just lost my best friend."

Amid his anguish and grief, Larry says it was his faith in God and Davey's outlook on life that inspired him to stay in racing. Davey had told Larry repeatedly that with God all things are possible and a person can endure anything. "Even if it just seems like it's the end of the world," Larry says, "if you put your faith in God, you're going to get through it. It may not be easy-peasy. It may not be easy street, but He promised He would not put more on us than we can take with His help." And so Larry put into practice what Davey had taught him. "There's nothing that can come my way today, including losing my best friend tragically, that God and I can't handle together."

Following Davey's tragic death, Larry's success as a crew chief with Robert Yates Racing continued with Ernie Irvan driving Davey's No. 28 Texaco-Havoline Ford to victory lane in back-to-back wins in Martinsville and Charlotte. And in

1994, Ernie finished second in the Daytona 500 and claimed back-to-back victories in Atlanta and Richmond. By August, Ernie and Dale Earnhardt Sr. were battling for the points championship. Then Michigan happened. Ernie wrecked into the wall during a practice run when his racecar's right front tire blew. "The worst thing that can happen as a crew chief is to ask your driver, 'Are you okay?' and to get no response," Larry says. "I remember just leaning over the wall and throwing up. How is this possible? How can this happen to us again?"

Doctors gave Ernie a 15 percent chance of survival from the head injuries he sustained in the crash. If not for a trackside physician who performed an emergency tracheotomy and opened Ernie's windpipe to prevent him from drowning in the blood hemorrhaging from his brain, he wouldn't have made it to the hospital alive. Three weeks later, Ernie miraculously came out of a medically-induced coma. And less than two years later, Ernie would be racing again. "One of the wins that was the most special was 1996 at Loudon, New Hampshire, when Ernie Irvan got back into victory lane," Larry says. "I felt like the weight of the world was gone off my shoulders because we had gotten that man back to victory lane." A couple of months later, the duo won again at Richmond.

A year later, Larry was hired by Richard Childress Racing to help seven-time NASCAR champion Dale Earnhardt Sr. win the Daytona 500, a race that had proven oddly elusive throughout the Hall of Fame driver's career. With seven top fives and 16 top tens, the No. 3 Goodwrench Chevrolet finished the season fifth in points but didn't win a race in 1997. The next year, Earnhardt finally won his first and only Daytona 500. Larry had accomplished what none of Earnhardt's previous pit crew chiefs could. And in unprecedented fashion, pit crew members from every competing race team lined pit road to high-five the Intimidator as he made his way to victory lane.

Larry spent two more winless seasons with RCR as crew chief for Mike Skinner before retiring in 2001 to join the FOX Sports television broadcast booth as the network's first crew chief analyst. During the first race of his inaugural season as a broadcaster, Larry witnessed the tragic death of Dale Earnhardt Sr. when his former driver crashed into the wall on Turn 4 of the race's final lap while running in third place behind Michael Waltrip and his son, Dale Earnhardt Jr.

"The wreck didn't look that bad," Larry recalls. "I kept keeping one eye on what was going on in Turn 4. And I think when I saw Kenny Schrader go over to the car and start waving his arms frantically, that was not a good sign, and when it really resonated with me that this probably was not good was when the ambulance left the scene and did not even stop at the infield care center, and just casually, slowly drove out of the Turn 4 tunnel, there didn't seem to be any sense of urgency. The most iconic driver, the Elvis Presley of NASCAR, was killed in a crash. Trust me, when that happened, safety innovation got accelerated in a big, big way. I think the sport knew, we all knew what Dale Earnhardt would want us to do, and that's what we did. We all went to Rockingham, North Carolina, and a few days later we did what we do. We raced."

In 2015, the 65-year-old transitioned from the broadcast booth to continue his work as an in-studio NASCAR analyst. After nearly 25 years as a broadcaster, Larry says he never imagined such a career for himself. "I figured when they were about ready to put me six feet under, I would be saying, 'Four tires next time.'" To be successful as both a crew chief and a broadcaster in the high-stakes world of stock car racing requires a lot of trust in your team—from the owner to the equipment haulers and everyone in between—to do their job as near perfect as possible. But most important, Larry says, is to trust God with the results. "One thing I never worry about is if I did everything I could do that day to do the best that I could do and be the best I could. I put it in God's hands. It's the plan He has and I'm okay with that. Just give it to Him. He's got a plan and just pray about it. It's going to be okay because, ultimately, all I really, really want is eternal life with Him at the end of this journey."

10

William Byron

From Virtual Reality to a Life of Authenticity

CALL IT A SIGN OF THE TIMES that William Byron, the pole setter for the 2023 NASCAR Cup Series championship race at Phoenix Raceway, got his start in the virtual racing world. "I got started with iRacing when I was 13 years old," he says. "The digital platform was pretty new to the NASCAR landscape and gave me a chance to have fun and learn how to drive. I'd never driven anything before, so iRacing gave me that entry into racing." For a lot of professional racecar drivers, their racing roots began on a dirt track when they were five or six years old and driving go-karts or something with two wheels and a motor. But William's childhood fascination with stock car racing began simply as a fan. By age 9, he had persuaded his dad to take him to see his first NASCAR race at Martinsville Speedway in what would become an annual father-son outing to attend races across the country. And throughout elementary and middle school, William's fandom for the sport became more intense.

In his first two iRacing seasons (2011–2012), William competed in 683 races—mostly from his home computer in his bedroom—winning 104 (15 percent) of them while collecting 203 top-five finishes. With his success, William's parents quickly realized that their financial support of their son's iRacing endeavors and beyond was worthwhile. At age 15, with only two months of experience driving a typical street car, William began driving on the Legends circuit, which utilizes 5/8-scale fiberglass versions of American cars from the 1930s and 1940s. That season he won 33 races and became the Legend Car Young Lions Division champion. In 2016, his only full season in the NASCAR Camping World Truck Series, William won seven races before moving to the Xfinity Series the following season. In 2017, he captured four Xfinity Series checkered flags, two pole positions, 12 top fives, 22 top tens, and Rookie of the Year en route to the championship with JR Motorsports. In 2018, he became the Cup Series Rookie of the Year and earned his first win at Daytona International Speedway in the iconic No. 24 Hendrick Motorsports Chevrolet Camaro ZL1 1LE.

Fast-forward to 2023 and William's No. 24 Chevy was among the fastest on the circuit. His six victories and average finish of 11.0 led all Cup Series regulars. The Charlotte native also established personal bests with 15 top fives, 21 top tens, and 1,016 total laps led. It took a gutsy performance in the Round of 8 finale at a hot Martinsville Speedway for William to advance to the championship race. William's helmet fan felt like a hair dryer as the temperature inside his vehicle reached triple digits. Even with blurry vision and a heart rate approaching 200 beats per minute, William refused to pit before finishing in 13th place to qualify for his first Championship 4 field at Phoenix Raceway. And it all happened at the same tight 0.526-mile oval where he saw his first NASCAR race with his dad in 2006. The same track where in April 2021 his mom became ill and was rushed to a local hospital for what was eventually diagnosed as MALT lymphoma, a treatable tumor on the side of her brain. In April 2022, William won the 500-lap, 263-mile race at Martinsville Speedway for the first time.

Starting on the pole at Phoenix Raceway, William led the championship race for the first 92 laps. And for 205 of 312 laps, he controlled the race within a race among the Championship 4 drivers. At the start of the final stage, William restarted second and held that position until Ryan Blaney passed him with 101 laps to go. He would finish the race in fourth, which was good enough for third place in the final 2023 Cup standings. "I think everyone in the Cup Series is just extremely talented, very good at what they do," William says. "And it takes every little detail to be competitive. So, I think for me, I just try to put as much work as I can into the things that I feel like matter towards performance, and it changes every year, but trying to just maximize every little detail."

William's unconventional route from iRacing to qualifying for the Cup Series playoffs every season since 2019 has shown that simulation racing can pave the way for future drivers to break into the sport on an actual track—especially after the digital platform took front and center for NASCAR when the COVID-19 pandemic shut down the sport in early 2020.

The eNASCAR iRacing Pro Invitational Series launched while the regular season was postponed because of the coronavirus outbreak. Television networks aired the simulation races during the times they had been scheduled to broadcast actual races. William won nearly half of the virtual races in that exhibition series before NASCAR resumed on-track racing in May without fans in the stands.

William's meteoric rise through the motor racing ranks comes with a faith perspective that keeps him centered and guides his priorities. He committed his life to Christ when he was 15 years old, about the same time his racing exploits went from virtual to reality. A few years later, William enrolled in Liberty University's online degree program, becoming an ambassador of sorts for the largest Christian university in the world when the Lynchburg, Virginia school became a major sponsor for his racecar. Liberty continues to be the primary sponsor for several of William's races each season. "There's a lot of Christians who are watching the races, and that Liberty University racecar represents something bigger than just the race," William says. "But you know, I just try to show my faith through the ways I feel empowered. So, I just try to be myself and live by the values that I know that God's instilled in me. I think really just keeping the right things at the center of what you do and keeping your faith at the center help make sure that you're keeping things in perspective." He also says having the right perspective for life on and off the track is key to not losing your identity and sense of what matters most. "The sport of NASCAR is really competitive. And there's tons of ups and downs. You have really high highs and really low lows, and you just have to kind of manage all that and stay true to the person you are. And I think also, for me, it's all about the people that I surround myself with. So just learning from them, their values, and sharing similar Christian values with the people I hang out with."

When conflicts arise, as they inevitably do in the heat of competition—like when a driver's split-second decision at 200 miles per hour sends dozens of other racecars simultaneously spinning out of control—perspective is everything. William says, "I think even last year [in 2022], just some of the conflicts that I had on the track, and things happen, and you're caught up in the emotions of it. But I think that managing those emotions and managing what you think is right—I think that really is what it comes down to, what you think is right, based on what you've learned through the Bible and through your faith and the people you surround yourself with. So, I think it's really important to make good decisions, moral decisions that you're proud of, and the people around you would be proud of. The thing I think about is trying to make decisions that are Christ-based. I want to be authentic to who I am. The biggest thing is that I have values that are faith-based, and I try to live by those to the best that I can, although I'm definitely not perfect."

11

Austin Dillon

The Joy of the Lord Is His Strength

IT'S RECOGNIZED AS ONE of the most harrowing and destructive wrecks in the history of NASCAR. And Austin Dillon, driver of the legendary No. 3 Richard Childress Racing Chevrolet, walked away from what was left of the inverted, mangled racecar after the entire hood section had been sheared from the frame. The checkered flag had barely waved on the July 5, 2015, Coke Zero 400 at Daytona International Speedway when Austin's 3,500-pound racecar went airborne from the bottom of the racetrack, then barrel-rolled over two rows of cars and up into the catch fence in front of the stands, before being flung upside down back onto the track and getting slammed by another racecar spinning out of control.

Looking back on that experience, Austin says, "It was one of the craziest wrecks in NASCAR history and destroyed the car, and definitely God took care of me then." He is also thankful for the sport's safety enhancements following the 2001 wreck at Daytona that killed Dale Earnhardt Sr., who had also been driving the No. 3 Chevrolet at the time.

Austin is even more thankful for the week that followed his death-defying crash. That's when he met his future wife, Whitney, at Kentucky Speedway, where he was remarkably deemed fit to race. "I think I'm more thankful now after being around for my wife," he says. "Her faith for God is just special. She definitely helps me in every facet of the things I do. She's a special woman. I'm very fortunate God put her in my life." Austin and Whitney, a former cheerleader with the NFL's Tennessee Titans, were engaged less than a year after their first meeting and were married in 2017. The couple have two young children—a son, Ace, and a daughter, Blaize—along with a French Bulldog named Gucci Girl. A few years ago, Austin and Whitney, along with their best friends, Paul and Mariel Swan (see chapter 32), opened their lives to the world in the USA Network reality show *Austin Dillon's Life in the Fast Lane*, which followed the two couples during the 2022 Cup Series. The show aired for one season, and Austin says it was a privilege to allow the world to see how much fun they have while seeking to honor God in all they do. "We set out as a group to be great representatives of God and shine His light any moment we had," Austin says. "Let's bring people to God with this show and let's make it be something cool. That is key. Bringing people to God is what matters the most, and being a good steward and representative on and off the track."

In August 2022, in the last race of the regular season, Austin won at Daytona to clinch the final spot in the Cup Series playoffs. That year he earned a career-best five top fives and 11 top tens, ending the season 11th in the Cup championship standings, which tied his best postseason performances from 2017 and 2020. Austin has so far won four Cup Series races, including the prestigious Daytona 500 in 2018. He has made the playoffs five times (2016–2018, 2020, 2022). He also has nine career wins in the Xfinity Series, where he claimed the 2013 championship. And he earned seven career wins and the 2011 championship in the Camping World Truck Series.

So how does a veteran, one who has competed at the highest level of stock car racing since 2014, respond after having the worst season of his career in 2023? That year Austin wound up 29th in points, with career-low numbers in average start (20.0), average finish (21.8), and did-not-finish (10). He also tied a career worst with only 20 lead-lap finishes. "Sometimes you might put in more effort, like in 2023—I feel like I put in more effort than I ever have and getting less from it than I ever have," he admits. "So, it's still a sport and you have to take it seriously every day. But also sometimes you've got to laugh and just enjoy the situation you're in and come out the other side and know that there's going to be a time where it's going to be your turn." Austin says he's discovered that when God is at the center of his life and family, then the results on the track aren't his true source of joy. "The lows are less low and the highs are a little less high when you have God in your life. That's why I'm so thankful for my family and our relationship with God, because there's a lot more bad days than good days in our sport, and if I let those determine the outcome of my days, it can be very lonely and dreary and woe-is-me."

Driving for RCR, owned by his grandfather and 2017 NASCAR Hall of Fame inductee Richard Childress, Austin relishes the responsibility he feels for carrying on the rich tradition and history of success that was born out of his grandfather's garage in 1969. RCR struggled for years before achieving sustained success, beginning in the mid-1980s with Dale Earnhardt Sr. behind the wheel. Today, the company has more than 300 team members, fields multiple Cup and Xfinity Series teams, and holds championships at every level of NASCAR.

While Austin grew up going to church and believing in God, he says that seeing the joy of the Lord in Whitney inspired him to recommit his life to Christ and be baptized before they got married. "I wanted to be like Whitney. She had a light about her. God put her in my life for a reason, and I'm thankful for that blessing." Since getting married, Austin says his love for the Bible and the privilege of prayer have transformed his life. One of his favorite verses is Romans 12:21: "Do not be overcome by evil, but overcome evil with good." "The key to it all," he professes, "is there's not one curveball that can't be answered in the Bible. It's all there. I think that prayer is key. Talk to God. Go to God for your answers. A lot of things that I take from the Bible are all answers to the hard questions in life. I'm a big believer in the power of prayer. So, find a good group of people that you can confide in and talk about God with."

Even now that he has his own family, Austin says he's also grateful for his father's continued spiritual influence on his life. Mike Dillon, who drove in the Xfinity Series in the mid-1990s, now serves as executive vice president for RCR. "My dad is unbelievable. We talk on Wednesday mornings after he has gotten up at 5 a.m. and reads his Bible. Being around people who push you to be better each and every day, and you can learn from them about what is most important in life, is extremely helpful. Iron sharpens iron."

12

Randall Burnett

The Most Important Question

AS THE CREW CHIEF for one of the winningest NASCAR drivers in the modern era, Randall Burnett's job is to have Kyle Busch's No. 8 Chevrolet Camaro ZL1 ready for whatever comes their way. Whether it's changing track conditions or mechanical issues that arise during a race, Randall's painstaking preparation and real-time adjustments are crucial to the team's success. "To be the guy that's responsible for making the decisions, whether it may be the car setup or aerodynamics or pit strategy or any of that, it's challenging and keeps me going," he says. "It's really gratifying."

When Busch left Joe Gibbs Racing to join the Richard Childress Racing team in Welcome, North Carolina, for the 2023 season, he and Randall won nearly immediately, scoring a victory at Auto Club Speedway in week 2 of the regular season. Kyle and Randall netted two other victories, including Talladega Superspeedway in April and World Wide Technology Raceway in June, which locked him into the playoffs for the 11th consecutive year. Kyle and Randall's 10 top fives and 17 top tens garnered them 14th place in the final points standings.

Growing up in Fenton, Missouri, Randall says he dreamed of being in the driver's seat instead of in the driver's ear. "I grew up racing go-karts with my dad. We raced every weekend somewhere. He worked hard all week, and we would pack up on Friday night and drive all night and go race somewhere Saturday, like Michigan or Wisconsin or New York, down here in Charlotte area, or whatever. We would go to all the big races."

Randall built and raced his own late models near his hometown and later attended the University of North Carolina Charlotte, where he earned a degree in mechanical engineering. "I didn't make it as a driver," he says. "I always wanted to do that. I had some good success when I was driving and won some races but just didn't have the right opportunity." Shortly after college, Randall started his NASCAR career with Chip Ganassi Racing, where he spent 10 years serving as a data acquisition engineer, lead race engineer, 7 post analysis engineer, and lead team engineer. He played a key role in the team's 2010 victories in the Daytona 500 and Brickyard 400, with driver Jamie McMurray capturing the checkered flag in both races. And in 2014, Randall worked closely with Kyle Larson during his rookie season, assisting his team in securing eight top-five and 17 top-ten finishes. By 2016, he got his first opportunity as crew chief in the Cup Series when he joined JTG Daugherty Racing and driver AJ Allmendinger. He led the team to two top fives and nine top tens, highlighted by a second-place finish at Martinsville.

A year later, Randall joined RCR as crew chief in the Xfinity Series, working with a variety of drivers. He and Matt Tift were teamed together in 2018 and made the series playoffs, finishing the season sixth overall in the final driver standings. Randall remained in the Xfinity Series in 2019 and was paired with Tyler Reddick. The pair collected six wins and won the series championship. The team was also incredibly consistent, racking up 24 top-five finishes in 33 races, with an average finish of sixth place. In 2020, Randall made the leap with Tyler to the Cup Series. Over the next three seasons, he built the team into a unit that consistently ran up front, scoring nine top tens in their first Cup season together, following that up in 2021 with 16 top tens and their first pole (Circuit of the Americas) before their breakout season in 2022. He finished that season with single-season career bests in wins (3), poles (3), and top fives (10) on the way to finishing 14th in the final driver standings. "So, making it as a crew chief to the highest level of NASCAR and being competitive and being fortunate enough to win races and have great drivers drive our cars, you know, that's a huge deal for me," he says.

For Randall, someone who makes a living not leaving anything to chance, it was a question from his fiancée that he couldn't answer that got him to do some serious soul-searching. He recalls, "We started talking about our future. We were talking about where do we see ourselves in five, 10, 15, 20 years. We talked about that and then DeAnna asked, 'Where do you see yourself after you pass? Where do you lie on that?' And that really got me thinking. I never really thought of it that way. We look at what's next in our day-to-day life, what's down the road near enough. And that kind of opened my eyes up a little bit. She questioned me about my faith in God."

Randall realized that he couldn't say with confidence whether he would spend eternity with God in heaven when he died. He thought about the transformation he had witnessed in his father after his parents divorced when he was in high school. He saw his dad faithfully attend church every week, something they never did when he was growing up. His dad fell in love with God's Word and would regularly invite Randall to attend church with him. When his father passed away from lung cancer in 2009, Randall felt confident that his dad was in heaven, but he didn't have that same assurance for himself. He had gone through a divorce before he met DeAnna and carried a lot of guilt from his failed marriage. But then he realized how God had used DeAnna in his life to help show him how Jesus desired a personal relationship with him like the one his father had discovered.

"I went through some hard times in my life and seemed to always come out better on the other side, and I knew that wasn't my doing," he says. "I feel like God was guiding me in a lot of decisions. Just from me racing and coming to grips with myself that I'm not going to be a professional racecar driver. So, what's my next move? So, for me to quit racing and go into just working on cars full-time—you know, how I've progressed and the opportunities that I've had through my career—I think learning more about my faith and my beliefs, really putting my faith in Jesus, in the Lord, I think it's helped me along the way." Now, Randall says, he has peace that only comes from knowing God has forgiven him and loves him unconditionally. He quotes Lamentations 3:25 as one of his favorite Bible verses: "The LORD is good to those whose hope is in him, to the one who seeks him" (NIV). "That kind of resonates with me," he says. "I've experienced that in my life."

13

Michael McDowell

Leading by Example

IN A SPORT DRIVEN BY BUMPER-BANGING, fender-bending, and side-swiping at speeds of nearly 200 miles per hour, this is a story about a veteran Cup Series driver who has garnered a reputation for putting Christ first during his nearly 20-year career. For 2021 Daytona 500 winner Michael McDowell, his first victory in 358 NASCAR starts was more about God's faithfulness en route to capturing the checkered flag on one of the most revered and celebrated racetracks in the world. "Considering the whole journey to winning the 500, I never felt like, 'Finally, I did it,'" Michael says. "I knew that God did it. I didn't do anything. I understand it's a big deal, but like it's a big deal when God provided this, this, this, this, this, and this."

A fiery crash finish among frontrunners Joey Logano and Brad Keselowski on the final lap of the race propelled Michael's No. 34 car from third to first, edging out reigning Cup champion Chase Elliott. "Brad started spinning right, Joey started spinning left, and there was just enough room for my car to squeeze through," Michael said in the postrace press conference. "It was like the seas parted and I was able to drive through the middle."[1]

But Michael's pursuit of racing started in a different direction. Growing up in Glendale, Arizona, he was on a fast track toward life in the fast lane. He started competing on BMX bikes as a three-year-old. Throughout his childhood, he piled up local, regional, national, and international championships at every level of the World Karting Association. His older brother partnered as his chief mechanic, and his parents were his wheels to the track nearly every weekend of the year. God was rarely mentioned during Michael's blue-collar upbringing. A strong work ethic, competitive spirit, respectful attitude, and responsible disposition were held in high esteem. But while grinding obsessively to be the best on the go-kart track, Michael's slow U-turn toward Christ began when he attended a friend's funeral and learned that heaven is not an award for being good.

Soon thereafter, a preacher's message about grace and God's offer of a fresh start and a clean slate with Jesus drove him to study the Bible for the first time as an 18-year-old. "And as I dug in more and more, God just revealed His truths to me," Michael says. "The God of the universe pursued me in a way that only He could."[2]

After Michael and his girlfriend, Jami, moved from Arizona to the Charlotte area so he could train as a stock car driver, the couple began attending a Bible study group at a new church start. Before long, they trusted Christ as Savior and repented of their sins, which in turn led them to the marriage altar in 2005. "Baptism for us was that symbolic act of coming out of the water and dying to self and dying to sin and coming to life in Christ, and being new and clean and fresh," he says.

Michael's transition to stock car racing appeared seamless after winning 2007 Rookie of the Year honors in the ARCA Series. But in 2008, his life was turned upside down—physically and spiritually—the day before the second race of his NASCAR Cup Series career at Texas Motor Speedway. That's when the 23-year-old lost control and accelerated into a safety barrier wall at more than 100 miles per hour during a prerace qualifying lap. The crumpled racecar erupted into flames and rolled like a barrel, flipping nearly a dozen times across the racetrack before landing upright. "It was nothing short of miraculous that I walked away," Michael recalls. "From that day forward, I was like, it's not about me. It's about making Jesus known. That was a transitioning point for me in my faith journey, where my career became more about living out my faith."

For the next 10 years, though, Michael struggled to secure his lane in NASCAR, bouncing from one underresourced team to another. When he failed to qualify for a race, he often worked as a motor coach driver or consulted for other teams in the hunt for a championship just to stay relevant in the sport. That might explain why his favorite Bible verse says, "Consider it pure joy, my brothers and sisters, whenever you face trials of many kinds, because you know that the testing of your faith produces perseverance" (James 1:2–3 NIV).

Before joining Front Row Motorsports in 2018 as the full-time driver of the No. 34 Ford, Michael considered walking away from his lifelong chase to race. Since then, however, his trajectory on the NASCAR circuit has risen with team owner and fellow Christian Bob Jenkins and primary team sponsor Love's Travel Stops. "It was hard," he says, "but God was shaping me and molding me and allowing me to have such great moments in life, even though the career wasn't great. Helping people come to the Lord and discipling, it was just so good."

Michael acknowledges that his personal convictions have cost him. "Millions of dollars, no doubt about it," he says. "I missed so many opportunities because I wouldn't drive something because of the sponsor. So many good opportunities that would have changed my career. No regrets. I think that your regrets in life are going to be being disobedient to what God's called you to do. I just know what I was called to do and not do."

Having amassed seven top-ten finishes in 20 races at Daytona International Speedway throughout his NASCAR career, Michael excitedly anticipated the 2021 Daytona 500. But he says his prerace prayer that day was unlike any other. Fighting back tears, Michael read the prayer he had journaled on his phone after reading the account in Mark 9 about a father's request for Jesus to heal his son. "I do believe, Lord. Help me to overcome my disbelief," Michael wrote regarding his chances to win the most coveted race of the season. "Jesus, You're the healer, provider. Help me believe that today all things are possible through You. All things . . . Rest for my soul, for my wife's soul. Victory in this race, safety in this race, I know that You hold it in Your hands. Guard my heart, soul, and mind. Give me the faith that can move mountains so that You can be honored and glorified."

Shortly before midnight, and nine hours after the green flag waved to start the race—including a rain delay of nearly six hours—Michael found himself in a strangely familiar position coming out of Turn 3 on the final lap. "I knew where I needed to be and I knew what I needed to do, and I feel that's supernatural too, like God prepared me for that moment," Michael says. "I pushed Brad [Keselowski]. Brad crashed Joey [Logano]. Everybody should be mad at me. Nobody's mad at me. They're mad at each other." After the race, Joey Logano, who had led the final 25 laps, had this to say about Michael's home stretch maneuver: "If we couldn't win, I'm really happy to see McDowell win this thing. He's a great guy, a great person, a good leader in life and has helped me a lot in my life, so it's very cool to see him win the Daytona 500."[3]

Michael says his legendary victories at Daytona in 2021 and at Indianapolis Motor Speedway in the 2023 Brickyard 200 pale in comparison to God's blessing him and Jami with four biological children and leading them on a seven-year international adoption process spanning three continents. Several years ago, the couple adopted a three-year-old boy from China who had been abandoned on the street at five days old after being born with a cleft hand and cleft feet.

"I know it's awesome and I don't want to downplay that," Michael says of the race wins. "I feel so grounded in the truth that the big deal is that God allowed me to experience it, and that God is faithful and that He walked with me through the whole process. God was good before the victories and, personally, I didn't need [the success]. God's given me a platform.

It's not for me to be famous, and it's not for me to be successful, and it's not for me to cash in on. It's for me to share His goodness and faithfulness. God can do anything He wants to do with us, if we're willing to hold things loosely. And I think that holding things loosely and walking in obedience go hand in hand."

After seven years with Front Row Motorsports, Michael is joining Spire Motorsports in 2025 on a multiyear contract.

Corey LaJoie

Putting Feet to Your Faith

YOU MIGHT THINK that as a third-generation racecar driver, Corey LaJoie was destined to compete in the NASCAR Cup Series. But strapping in the No. 7 Spire Motorsports Chevrolet Camaro ZL1 is not something the Charlotte native ever takes for granted. The rise to stock car racing's premiere division has been a journey full of starts, stops, spins, and turns.

Corey started driving go-karts at age 3 and won his first race at 13. As the son of Randy LaJoie, two-time NASCAR Xfinity Series champion, and grandson of Don LaJoie, a member of the New England Auto Racing Hall of Fame, Corey grew up around the garage and racetrack. "I've had my fair share of humble pie," Corey says. "I see my trajectory, up and down, out of the sport and then back as a crew chief before getting behind the wheel again. My path is what it is because God has me right where He wants me to be."

Growing up in a Christian racing family meant church on Sundays looked different for the LaJoies. Thankfully for them and the many others who make a living in the fast lane nearly 40 weekends out of the year, there's been Motor Racing Outreach, an evangelical ministry to stock car racing teams for more than 30 years. It was this family of faith—made up of team owners, drivers, pit crew members, and their spouses and children—where Corey learned the importance of pursuing God's plan for his life. An MRO-sponsored mission trip to Costa Rica opened 15-year-old Corey's eyes to a world in great need. Ever since that mission trip, Corey hasn't been able to rid his mind of the images of poverty-stricken men, women, boys, and girls who can't even afford a pair of shoes.

That's why in the summer of 2019, when his No. 32 Ford, owned by Go Fas Racing, desperately needed a sponsor in order to qualify to compete at Watkins Glen International Speedway in New York, Corey couldn't help but think about those far less fortunate than him. One restless night about 11:30, his mind raced while lying in bed and staring at the ceiling fan as it circled like cars whipping around an oval asphalt track. "I know this sounds a little crazy," Corey told Kelly, his newly wedded wife, "but I think we should donate a month's salary for Samaritan's Feet to sponsor our racecar at Watkins Glen." Since 2003, Samaritan's Feet has provided shoes for more than 8.7 million people across 109 countries and 530 US cities.[1]

After a midnight call to his race team's owner to confirm his plans to forgo a month's salary to raise funds for the humanitarian organization, Corey promised to write on his racecar the name of every person who made a financial donation of any amount to the Hope Givers page on the Samaritan's Feet website. He and Kelly hoped to raise $20,000 for the nonprofit. But by the time Corey started his engine for the 90-lap road course, his car was covered with the names of 1,800 donors who had raised $135,000—enough to purchase 5,400 pairs of shoes.

Corey likens his prerace sponsorship dilemma to the account in Matthew 14 of the lad who donated the two fish and five loaves that Jesus multiplied to feed over 5,000 people. "It's human nature to hold on to what you think you can control," Corey says. But the race at Watkins Glen taught him a lesson about God's faithfulness that he'll never forget. "God can do the miracle, but you've got to step off the boat first." A month later, Corey again rallied donors to support Samaritan's Feet during the September race in Charlotte and raised an additional $75,000. He admits he could not have taken such a bold step of faith and donated a month's salary to charity in the midst of his team's own funding challenges without trusting and obeying God's Word. Corey likes to quote James 1:22, which reminds us, "Do not merely listen to the word, and so deceive yourselves. Do what it says" (NIV).

It was another MRO-led mission trip that changed Corey's perspective about the importance of daily prayer and Bible study. On day 6 of a 12-day mission to Haiti, Corey's curiosity was piqued about MRO chaplain Nick Terry's love for God's Word. "How often do you read that thing?" Corey inquired. Before long, Corey was enjoying his own daily 15-minute devotional in the Scriptures. He says, "The more you read the Bible, the more you want to read it. It really turns into your daily bread. You can't live without it because your soul hungers for it. It's easy to say the right thing and put on a facade on social media, but the only person that knows your heart is the Lord."

What once seemed intimidating and difficult for Corey, daily Bible reading, is now the difference between his merely knowing about God and truly knowing Him. And as Kelly followed her husband's lead, she soon realized her need to know Jesus Christ as her Savior and Lord. Following Kelly's profession of faith in Christ, she and Corey were baptized together in the ocean in 2019. The couple's newfound spiritual bond was strengthened a year later when their first child, Levi, was born five weeks prematurely. During Levi's two-week hospitalization, the couple said their faith in God was strengthened by His promises in Proverbs 3:5–6: "Trust in the LORD with all your heart, and do not lean on your own understanding. In all your ways acknowledge him, and he will make straight your paths."

Corey says the title of his podcast, *Stacking Pennies*, embodies his mission to faithfully pursue God's plans and purposes for his life one decision at a time, one day at a time while he continues to chase his first NASCAR Cup Series victory. "A penny seems insignificant, but once you start getting a couple and you can stack them on top of each other, they actually make something that's quantifiable and you can actually do something useful," he says. "That applies to everything, right? It's just little details you do in life that all add up in the future to something. Everything you do is going to compound, whether it's good or bad. I've chased worldly things and realize that at the end of the day, the only thing that brings continued happiness and contentment is my faith in Jesus. To work as though you're working for the Lord and not for man is certainly something that I try to keep in perspective."

15

Jeremy Clements

Trusting God in Your Darkest Hour

EVERY TIME JEREMY CLEMENTS starts the engine of his No. 51 Chevrolet Camaro for an Xfinity Series race, he feels like a winner. Never mind that the odds makers give him little to no chance of finishing in the top five when the checkered flag falls. As a family-owned race team, Jeremy Clements Racing doesn't have the resources and financing of the larger multi-driver NASCAR teams that are rich in corporate sponsorships and stocked with equipment and personnel. But for the Spartanburg, South Carolina native, it's always been the competitive challenge that drives him to defy the odds. And every time he straps himself in the driver's seat to compete in NASCAR's second-tier series, that's exactly what he does. With nearly 500 green flags under his belt in the Xfinity Series,

Jeremy ranks among the top five drivers of all time for most race starts. And yet some feared that his professional racing career was over before it barely got started.

In 2004, doctors at Wake Forest University Baptist Hospital told Jeremy he would never race again after the drive shaft exploded through the sheet metal into his super late model racecar and nearly severed his right hand. "I was racing down the front stretch at about 120 miles per hour and there was an explosion, and I look down and my right hand is barely hanging on my arm," he says. "I just pulled over. We were probably five laps from the finish too. And that was just a bad night." Surgeons initially recommended amputating Jeremy's hand, but his father insisted they do everything possible to save it.

After a nine-hour surgery, Jeremy's right hand was successfully reattached, and nine more surgeries would follow over the next year. All the while, Jeremy had one request of his doctors. He told them, "I just need you to make it hold a steering wheel." Bone and tendon grafts from his hip and foot were used to rebuild his hand. At one point, doctors even sewed his hand to his side for a month to help skin grafts attach successfully. Amazingly, after a year of therapy, Jeremy was back racing on dirt short tracks like 311 Speedway in Madison, North Carolina, where his racing dreams had nearly died when he was just 19. "My passion has always been racing," he says. "I was devastated. I'm thinking the world's over and they're telling me I'm doomed, and I'm just like, there's got to be a way. It was hell for a year. I mean, it was tough. And it was surgeries and physical therapy and just something I wouldn't wish on anybody."

Jeremy began racing go-karts when he was seven years old. Throughout his childhood and teenage years, he amassed dozens of championship trophies that now collect dust inside the 5,000-square-foot shop that houses the family's racing business. The shop was built in 1974 by his grandfather Crawford, a former NASCAR team owner and engine builder who also was a crew chief for Junior Johnson, Buck Baker, and A.J. Foyt in the early 1960s. Today, Jeremy's dad, Tony, builds the racing engines and serves as his crew chief. Since going full-time in the Xfinity Series in 2011, Jeremy has won two races—a road course in 2017 at Road America in Wisconsin and a superspeedway race at Daytona in August 2022. "We race probably on only one-eighth of a NASCAR team's race day budget," Jeremy says. "I want to show that we're a competitive team. Yes, we are small, but we can get the job done for a lot less money."

In a sport that's built on speed but is ironically a test of endurance, Jeremy is quick to credit his faith in God as the reason for his perseverance over the years. "When I was a first or second grader, I remember doing the prayer and asking the good Lord to come into my heart. And I don't know any other way." Jeremy admits that he wonders how his life might have been different if his Xfinity career hadn't been delayed by his life-changing accident. "It was very tough to understand why this happened to me," he says. "But I don't blame God whatsoever. I mean, it's just part of the journey I was put through. At first, I had some ill will towards God, but then I got over that and believed He's going to get me through this. And I need to just trust in the process. And looking back, I'm glad that I did not waver in my faith."

Nearly every week, Jeremy has an opportunity to see God provide. Whether it's finalizing a sponsorship or rebuilding a wrecked racecar, each day has challenges that must be met.

And Jeremy doesn't like to face those challenges without first talking to God. "I try to read the Bible every morning as I drink my coffee," he says. "The Bible says tell Him what you need. So, I just try to spell it out and talk to the good Lord like He's my heavenly Father. He's my friend. He knows everything about me anyway. He knows what I'm wanting and needing, but I tell Him anyway. He does bless us for sure."

And sometimes God shows Himself "able to do far more abundantly than all that we ask or think" (Eph. 3:20). Avoiding costly crashes and finishing in the top 10 or 12 usually makes for a good day at the racetrack for JCR. But with God, anything is possible, Jeremy says. Like his win at Daytona. "If you go back and watch that race, I mean we should have been in numerous crashes," he says. "The crash at the end took out more than a dozen cars and we were literally right in the middle of it until I drove on the high side of the track where nobody touched me. Going into Daytona, I didn't even look at that race like it was a race we could possibly win. Those races are survival to me. You never know when you're going to win again. And that's what keeps me going because I love to compete. I love racing. I love to win. And I guess I'm just always very hopeful."

And why shouldn't he be? Jeremy is still defying the odds— one prerace prayer at a time. "'Thank you for saving my hand and for the opportunity to race today,' so that's always the first thing I say, even to this day. All this time later."

16

Matt DiBenedetto

The Night That Changed Everything

IN 2020, Matt DiBenedetto experienced his most success-ful season of Cup Series racing. As the driver of the No. 21 Ford for Wood Brothers Racing, Matt was the runner-up in the second race of the season at Las Vegas Motor Speedway and tallied nearly a dozen top-ten finishes to qualify for the playoffs before finishing the season 13th in the points standings. Yet despite his success on the track, Matt was desperately searching for answers outside the racecar. He felt empty, anxious, and discontent. His marriage was strug-gling. And the chaos and uncertainty of the COVID-19 pan-demic had him questioning the meaning and purpose of his life.

Meanwhile, for some time, Matt had been observing a humble confidence and joyful peace exuding from fellow NASCAR driver and friend Michael McDowell. So, one weekend before a race in Richmond, Virginia, Matt approached Michael with a question. "I just said, 'Hey, man, how do you view all this stuff, all that's happening in the world, from your faith perspective?'" Michael's response immediately gripped Matt's heart and mind. "It was like God spoke right through that man to me," Matt says. "He said, 'Death has been defeated. I know who wins. I know how the story ends.' And when he told me that, I knew that he knew. He didn't just have some religious belief. He was 100 percent absolute with every fiber of his being all the way down to his soul and his spirit. And so, it drove me crazy in a good way. I've got to know like he actually knows, so I didn't care about religion or any of that. I just wanted to know the truth."

Matt describes himself at that time as "the most Bible-illiterate person you could meet." He had grown up in California and raced on dirt tracks since he was seven years old. At 13, his family moved to Hickory, North Carolina, where he started racing on asphalt tracks while advancing through the ranks in pursuit of his life's ambition to compete in the NASCAR Cup Series. Ironically, following his sixth Cup season, the most successful of his professional career, Matt says he was the most miserable and disillusioned he had ever been. "Jeremiah 29:13 says, 'You will seek me and find me, when you seek me with all your heart.' I was finally very open-hearted and seeking God with everything in me. Nothing else mattered. I only wanted to know the truth about life, and nothing else was really on my radar. I'm an all-in kind of guy to a fault, but this was the one thing I'm glad I was all in on. I was on a hunt and a search, and I was going to find the living God or I was going to die trying."

Matt spent about a month researching, watching You-Tube videos of Bible studies and sermons and reading the Bible. While online, he found Living Waters, the ministry of Christian apologist and evangelist Ray Comfort. There he learned about how God's holiness and justice demand that a perfect sacrifice be made for the forgiveness of sin—that is, disobedience to God's law, the Ten Commandments. The evangelist's teachings that Jesus Christ, God's perfect Son, endured His Father's righteous wrath and judgment of sin by dying on a cross so that sinners can be forgiven helped Matt begin to realize how much God loves him. He finally understood that Jesus's sacrificial death and victorious resurrection from the grave meant that eternal life in heaven is available to anyone who repents of their sins and professes Christ as their Savior and Lord. "I was really frustrated because I needed to know 100 percent where I'm going when I die," Matt says. "I needed to know, not just hope for the best on the other side. I was sitting on my couch about midnight, and I was just really distraught and had a lot of nerves and anxiety and things overcoming me, and then it hit me like a ton of bricks: I've got to understand what I was truly saved from. I had the love of God and the fear of God immensely put into me all in one moment. And I got to understand and feel it all the way down to my core, what eternal separation from God was."

He describes his experience as a spiritual awakening. "I just cried out to God, 'I've got to know You. I'll give You all of me.' I wasn't praying fancy prayers. I didn't know much about the Bible. I just knew enough and my heart was in the right place. I knew that Jesus was real, and I knew that He died for my sins and rose again. I was starting to understand just the basics of God's story and that I needed to know that He defeated death, my greatest enemy. So then when I cried out to Him, He heard me as He always does, and He made His presence known. I realized in one instant what it meant to be born again. His Holy Spirit came over me. His presence washed over me. I felt peace, joy, love. It was like He met me in my living room and wrapped His arms around me and gave me the tightest hug I've ever felt in my whole life."

Overwhelmed with joy, Matt awakened his wife, Taylor, who was fast asleep in their bedroom. "I told her, 'I just met Jesus. He's real and I just gave my life to Him.' So, we prayed together for the first time that night." Matt credits Taylor, who has been a Christian since before they got married in 2017, with patiently praying for him for years to receive God's grace and forgiveness. "I started realizing how much in my personal life I was blinded by my own self pride in so many ways. My wife and I were immediately on the same page. Ultimately, God was getting me and my wife together to be more obedient to Him and to listen to Him." The couple celebrated their newfound union in Christ as husband and wife by being baptized in their home swimming pool. Michael McDowell officiated the baptism as friends and family celebrated their public professions of faith.

But little did Matt know when he became a Christian how much his faith would anchor and guide him in the days ahead as his NASCAR career took an unexpected turn. Wood Brothers released him at the end of the 2021 season. After seven seasons at the Cup Series level, Matt had nine top fives and 31 top tens in 248 starts, achieving a best result of second in the 2019 Night Race at Bristol. He also won the NASCAR All-Star Open at Bristol in July 2020. "I really had to lean into God and trust that His plans are always right," Matt says. "I got humbled a lot and it was a big blessing. Being in the Truck Series, it was kind of like a reset for me. God has helped me to really have a much better appreciation for racing and for what I get to do for a living. God was using it all for good to get me to trust Him and to spew a lot of darkness, a lot of strongholds, out of my life through a lot of tough tests and trials. I've learned to listen more in life in general and especially listen to God."

During the 2022 and 2023 seasons, Matt competed full-time in the Craftsman Truck Series for Rackley W.A.R. He earned his first career NASCAR win in the Truck Series race at Talladega Superspeedway in October 2022. For the 2023 season, Matt had two top fives and 12 top tens en route to securing the team's first playoff berth and a 10th-place finish in the points standings. But after his elimination from the playoffs, Matt decided to end his association with the No. 25 Chevrolet Silverado to explore other racing opportunities. The 2024 season saw Matt return to the Xfinity Series as driver for the upstart Viking Motorsports team.

"God's definitely shown me just to trust in Him and His plan," Matt testifies. "And I've learned to take more of the passenger seat in life, and it's so much more peaceful knowing that God is steering the ship of my life. And so, I think I can take the passenger seat and trust Him. As long as I know I'm doing everything in my control to the best of my ability, all the stuff that's out of my control is truly in God's hands.

And it's nice when you just work in unity and fellowship and friendship with God and trust Him, knowing that I'm doing my part. God's always doing His part. So, it just brings such a peace beyond comprehension, a peace I didn't even know was attainable in life."

17

Grant Enfinger

Finding Contentment Where You Are

AT 38, GRANT ENFINGER finally made his NASCAR Cup Series debut in June 2023 at Sonoma Raceway. So, it seemed only fitting that he started in 35th position at the hilly, 12-turn, 2.52-mile California road course. After all, the track couldn't be more symbolic of Grant's journey to stock car racing's premier series. But to say that Grant's opportunity to race on Sunday was a long time coming wouldn't be entirely accurate. He actually had less than a week to prepare to drive Legacy Motor Club's No. 42 Chevrolet Camaro in the Toyota/Save Mart 350.

"Me and my wife prayed a lot beforehand," he says. "She could tell that I was very stressed. It was like two days to prepare for this. So, it was definitely a little bit overwhelming to that point, but once it actually started, it was fun." Grant's wife, Michelle, also encouraged him to enjoy the opportunity while he had it. Throughout his career, Grant has made the most of his opportunities. After graduating in 2007 with a degree in marketing from the University of South Alabama, he spent most of the next decade honing his craft in the ARCA Series, winning a championship in 2015. He joined the Truck Series full-time in 2017 and led the regular season standings two years later.

But the Next Gen car in the Cup Series is quite different from the racecars that Grant drove to his 16 ARCA and 10 Truck Series victories. The aerodynamics, fuel mileage, seating, gear shifting, turning, braking, and tire traction in the Next Gen car all make for an unprecedented driving experience. Combine that with a crowded road course at 80 miles per hour, and Grant felt like a rookie driver again. But when it came time to find a replacement for Noah Gragson, who was sidelined with a concussion, Legacy knew that Grant was up for the challenge. Their relationship through GMS Racing dated back to 2015 when Grant won the ARCA Menards Series Championship in the No. 23 Chevy. The following year, he won his maiden Truck Series race with the team at Talladega in his part-time schedule.

In 2023, Grant was driving the No. 23 Champion Power Equipment Chevrolet on the NASCAR Craftsman Truck Series for GMS Racing, which was owned by Legacy. With the Truck Series not racing that weekend, Legacy recruited Grant to fill Noah's seat in their Cup car. And when the checkered flag dropped, Grant had finished a respectable 26th—nine positions higher than he started.

The Fairhope, Alabama native got his racing start in go-karts at age 11. After competing in the Legend and Late Model divisions locally, Grant crawled into the national racing tour. He made 18 ARCA starts over a three-year period before his first full season in 2011. Then he started only 14 ARCA races over the next three seasons before getting another full-time ride. Grant toiled in the truck racing series with only 14 races across a seven-year period before a full-time opportunity finally opened the door in 2017 when he was 32. After stringing together several one-year contracts with various teams, Grant concluded a two-year contract with GMS Racing by finishing runner-up in the 2023 Truck Series championship standings with three wins, nine top fives, and 13 top tens.

Grant says that he's learned some of his greatest lessons in life behind a steering wheel. "I was a teenager when I would start driving my granddad to church. Whenever I had a faith question or a question about God or questions about life, we would talk about it. Or if I didn't have anything, he would just tell you kind of plain as day what you're doing right and what you're doing wrong." Grant's grandad was a Methodist preacher and highly respected in his family and community. "It was more just like seeing him live his life and seeing the respect that I have for him and that other people have for him," Grant says. "And just something about him in the way he carried himself, that's more or less what brought me to know Christ." Grant says his faith and maturity in his relationship with Christ have grown the most since he married Michelle nearly 10 years ago. "I feel like since being married and my wife being a Christian, we work together to be in the Word more often. We are more bold in our faith. I'd say for a long time, I was more of a casual Christian."

A few years ago, Grant came to realize that his happiness and fulfillment in life were too dependent on his racing career.

At the end of the 2020 season, after qualifying for his first Championship 4 finale in the Truck Series, Grant was demoted to part-time status when ThorSport Racing split his 2021 race schedule with another driver. Somehow, winning four races in one season and competing for a championship wasn't enough to secure Grant's status as his team's primary driver. "I thought everything was hunky dory with the team," he says. "It was more of a crossroads probably in my career."

That same year, Grant also drove for CR7 Motorsports in nine races and finished in the top 10 three times, including a memorable fourth-place finish at Circuit of the Americas road course in Austin, Texas. Having to drive for two different teams in 2021 changed Grant's perspective about what matters most. He says, "Christ is more important than what's going on in my racing world or career. And that was probably one of the bigger moments in my life that I got through that year." As of the 2024 season, Grant is grateful to find himself back with CR7 Motorsports. And this time he has a multiyear contract to drive the No. 9 Chevrolet Silverado in the Craftsman Truck Series. "The racing industry is so volatile and so up and down. And there's so many moments that you feel like you're on top of the world, and there's so many moments that you are in the very bottom. A lot of times, it can change over the course of a few weeks. I've learned that racing isn't the cure all, end all, be all—God is, Jesus is."

18

Bobby and Kristin Labonte

*Stewarding Your Platform
for God's Purposes*

WHEN BOBBY LABONTE won NASCAR's 2000 Winston Cup Series Championship in Joe Gibbs Racing's No. 18 Chevy Monte Carlo, the euphoria of reaching the pinnacle of stock car racing faded nearly as quickly as the smoke after his victory burnout.

"I remember calling Coach [Gibbs] the day after we won the championship and saying, 'I thought there would be more to this,'" Bobby shared during his 2020 Hall of Fame induction speech. "And just as he had done so many times before, he taught me another life lesson. He reminded me, 'It's not about the win or the title. It's about the journey and the experiences to get there.'"[1]

Bobby's journey to NASCAR's heights began in the late 1960s as a child racing quarter midgets on 1/20-mile banked oval dirt and asphalt tracks in south Texas. Eight years younger than his brother, Terry, Bobby was inspired to follow his older brother's passion for motorsports. In the 1980s, when the Labonte family moved from Corpus Christi, Texas, to North Carolina to help Terry chase his NASCAR dreams, Bobby was all in for the ride. It wouldn't be long before he began immersing himself in the sport wherever he could— from sweeping garage floors to helping on pit road. Bobby and his father, Bob, helped work on the team owned by Billy Hagan that Terry won his first Cup Series championship with in 1984. But two years later, when Terry left Hagan Racing to drive for NASCAR Hall of Famer Junior Johnson, Bobby started his own late model team and began racing full-time with his father as crew chief. The 23-year-old won multiple races across the Carolinas en route to a championship in 1987. By 1991, Bobby claimed the Grand National Series (now the Xfinity Series) championship over future NASCAR Hall of Famer Jeff Gordon, while driving a racecar that he owned himself.

The following year, Bobby lost the Busch Grand National Series title to Joe Nemechek by just three points. But his impressive results garnered him his first full-time Cup Series opportunity with Bill Davis Racing in 1993. That fall he earned his first career Cup Series pole at Richmond, Virginia, and finished second to Jeff Gordon for the season's Rookie of the Year honors. Two years later, he joined Joe Gibbs Racing to take over for Dale Jarrett in the famed No. 18 Interstate Batteries car. Bobby won his first Cup Series race that Memorial Day weekend in the series' longest event, the Coca-Cola 600 at Charlotte Motor Speedway. In 1999, he finished runner-up to Dale Jarrett in the Cup championship and then captured the 2000 Cup title with a 265-point advantage over seven-time champion Dale Earnhardt Sr. Bobby's run of dominance on the racetrack had him finishing eighth or better in the championship points standings from 1997 through 2003. Over his Cup Series career, he won 21 races at 11 different tracks, and 26 pole positions at 16 different tracks. Interestingly, his last pole position came in his home state at Texas Motor Speedway.

Of all the racing legends that Bobby has competed against, some of the most special for him are the battles with his two-time Cup champion brother. And at the top of that list of races is the Cup season finale at Atlanta Motor Speedway in 1996 when Bobby won the race and Terry, who finished fifth, clinched his second Cup title. They celebrated by taking a victory lap together. The Labonte brothers are only the second pair of siblings to be inducted into the NASCAR Hall of Fame, joining Glen and Leonard Wood.

But Bobby says the journey is more important than the wins and championships that landed him in the Hall of Fame. That journey is highlighted by the steady Christian influence that he experienced while working with Joe Gibbs and Norm Miller, former president of Interstate Batteries, which was JGR's primary sponsor. "Just being around Coach Gibbs and Norm Miller, and that whole team was a different aspect for me in my life," says Bobby, who didn't grow up going to church very often. "It was really easy for me to see how Joe and Norm raised their kids and lived their lives and led by example. Their faith is what intrigued me and helped me understand that it's not about me."

Another life-changing part of the journey for Bobby was attending chapel services led by chaplains with Motor Racing Outreach before the Sunday races. "So, when I started going to church on Sundays before the race, that's when I gave my life to Christ," he says. And then driving his No. 18 racecar took on an eternal purpose when the phrase "John 3:16" was emblazoned on the right rear quarter of his green-and-black Pontiac and an advertisement for the 2004 cinematic debut of *The Passion of the Christ* covered the hood.

Even though he's now retired from NASCAR, Bobby and his wife, Kristin, are as committed as ever to leveraging their platform for God's glory. At 60, Bobby is a kidney cancer survivor and a television analyst for NASCAR on FOX. He also competes in the Modified Tour and Superstar Racing Experience on short tracks around the country. Kristin, a three-time US Masters Cycling National Champion and former professional cyclist, has competed for some of the premier American professional cycling teams and for the USA National Team from 2000 to 2012. She is president of Breaking Limits, a brand strategy, experiential marketing, and communications agency that Bobby founded in 2007, specializing in the motorsports arena. Kristin also leads the Bobby Labonte Foundation, providing strategic vision and leadership to the organization, which has raised over $1 million for children and families. "We feel like we have been given a platform and we need to use it," Kristin says. "We've been given gifts. And it's up to us to do the very best we can with those gifts. Those gifts are not ours. We can't take credit for them. They're gifts from God that He put in us and that He instills in us every day. So, it's up to us to do the very best we can to glorify God because everything that we have comes from Him. And everything that we get to do is because of Him, and so we need to make sure that we are walking the walk."

19

Don Hawk

When Your Career Becomes God's Calling

AS DON HAWK SAT at a banquet table alongside 1986 Winston Cup Rookie of the Year Alan Kulwicki, he had no idea that an executive career in NASCAR spanning four decades was in his future. At the time, Don worked for a conglomerate of Ford dealerships in the Northeast that sponsored Alan's independently owned race team as well as Wood Brothers Racing. "I've been either in the automobile business or racecar business my entire working life," Don says. "In high school, I was at the racetrack Saturday and Sunday. I was one of the youngest guys that was a car dealership lot attendant because I could drive a car without a license. My brother-in-law worked there as a used car manager. He's the one that introduced me to racing when I was about eight years old. And he used to race and I'd go to the racetrack with him. But he taught me how to drive a car when I was nine years old. I drove a pickup truck. When I was 12 years old, I could drive a tow truck."

Don's obsession with all things automotive was challenged in the summer of his junior year in high school. He attended a revival meeting in Zionsville, Pennsylvania, with some friends on the Fourth of July. The following evening they returned. "At the end of the service, I couldn't help but say, 'I am a sinner who needs a Savior,'" Don recalls. "And so, I went forward to make a decision for Christ, and amazingly, to my right and to my left, was my mother, my father, and my older sister. They were at the same camp meeting, and we didn't even know it. They felt compelled to go forward that same night. It was almost household salvation, but I had another sister who did not attend the revival meeting." Don's profession of faith in Christ awakened a hunger to study the Bible. After graduating from high school, he attended Philadelphia College of the Bible where he majored in biblical studies. Don was voted by his graduating class as most likely to continue his studies at Dallas Theological Seminary before returning to serve on the faculty of his alma mater.

But Don says that's where his path took a different turn. "I wanted to put my ministry to work in the marketplace. I just decided that I didn't want to go for four more years of education. I wanted to get to work and be an impact in a Christlike fashion." Fast-forward a decade to when Don and his wife, Cyndee, were Alan's guests at the NASCAR awards banquet. Don was in his early 30s, a father of four, and a novice to the business side of stock car racing. But he was more than eager to learn while continuing in the automobile dealership industry. So, he spent the next six years helping

Alan Kulwicki Racing grow the business while remaining off the payroll.

By 1992, Alan was a Winston Cup Series champion and Don had left the automobile dealership to be the full-time manager of AKR. Tragically, Alan was killed the night of April 1, 1993, when the twin-engine plane he was in crashed into a rural hillside near Blountville, Tennessee. The pilot and two other passengers on board the plane also died. Alan had been scheduled to race at Bristol Motor Speedway two days later. Suddenly, Don found himself helping settle Alan's estate.

Before long, Don received a dinner invitation from Dale Earnhardt Sr. who was looking for someone to lead the launch of his new company, Dale Earnhardt, Inc. They agreed to kick the tires on the idea and see if they would be a good fit for each other. "I traveled with him for a month," Don says. "During that month he actually won three races—one Busch Grand National race and two Cup races. And he joked with me as we got on an airplane after we won at Pocono that I must be a good luck charm." As president of DEI from 1993 to 2000, Don helped build the company from the ground up, including assembling three Cup teams, a Grand National team, and a Truck Series team. Along the way, the company launched a racing souvenir company for the seven-time Cup Series champion. "We also won a lot of big races together and did a lot of big business deals together," Don says. "So, I took the road less traveled by and that's made all the difference. I really believe that to be true."

Don left DEI to launch Hawk Sports Management six months before Dale lost his life in the 2001 Daytona 500 crash. He says, "I have learned to play the hand you're dealt. And sometimes you're going to lose and sometimes it's going to hurt. Sometimes you're going to cry. Sometimes you're going to need help. Sometimes you're going to need prayer."

In the early 2000s, Don was hired by NASCAR to serve as director of regional racing development before joining Speedway Motorsports, LLC in 2007. SM owns 11 racetracks across the country that host nearly a third of NASCAR's Cup, Xfinity, and Craftsman Truck Series racing schedule each year. During his 14-plus years there, Don served in a number of executive roles, including vice president of business affairs and chief racing development officer. Don's close working relationship with SM founder Bruton Smith, who also built Charlotte Motor Speedway, afforded him the opportunity to encourage Bruton in his faith when he was in failing health near the end of his life. "I used to accompany Bruton most everywhere he went on business," Don recalls. "When he got very, very sick and became wheelchair-bound and reached the point where he couldn't fly in his private plane anymore or go to the races, I would visit him regularly at his house." And when Bruton faced life-threatening cancer surgery, Don was by his side. "We held hands and we prayed, and he rededicated his life to Christ."

When Don moved out of his office overlooking Charlotte Motor Speedway in 2021, the Pottstown, Pennsylvania native was only out of a job for a few weeks before becoming CEO of the Superstar Racing Experience. The short-track competition featured 11 current and former NASCAR all-star drivers and one local driver. In the summer of 2022, CBS broadcasted the six-race series on Saturday nights, and ESPN would broadcast the 2023 season to rave reviews. "I got the joy of the journey of being the CEO and putting the pieces of the puzzle together," Don says.

As for his future, the 69-year-old grandfather of 13 references Jesus's words from Luke 12:48 as his life's mission: "Everyone to whom much was given, of him much will be required, and from him to whom they entrusted much, they will demand the more." Don testifies, "Life has been more abundant to me than I could ever ask. To whom much is given, much is required. I've got to continue to pay it forward. I was in debt upside down and Jesus paid it forward for me. I've got to do whatever I can in a business sense and godly giving sense. Not just tithing but being charitable and kind. I've been blessed with much spiritually, emotionally, financially, and physically."

20

Ty and Haley Dillon

How God Saved Our Marriage

SUCCESS HAD FOLLOWED Ty Dillon everywhere. So when he began racing full-time in the NASCAR Cup Series in 2017, he expected the same. Running up front had become commonplace for him while winning the ARCA Series championship in 2011 before his 20th birthday. Over the 2012 and 2013 seasons, Ty won a combined total of three races in the Truck Series and finished in the top five in the season point standings both years while driving for his grandad and Hall of Fame owner Richard Childress. Across those two seasons, Ty claimed 16 top fives and 29 top tens in the Truck Series. From 2014 through 2016, Ty finished in the top five in the season point standings at the Xfinity Series level. But a couple of seasons into the Cup Series, Ty's view of the track was consistently from the back of the pack. "I went from being a guy who was at the top of every race to near the bottom, which for me was a mind flip. I was battling depression and thoughts of like, 'Man, I don't care if I hit the wall and I don't get out of the car.' Like, it was as deep as that at points. On the outside, it looked as though I was on top of the world racing in the Cup Series, but inside I just couldn't see a future for myself. I couldn't see how I was going to pull out of this."

For years, Ty's identity had been driven by his results in a racecar. "I put my self-worth into what other people thought of me, and it was easy to do that and it was rewarding when you were winning all the time. And then it was not rewarding, and I just kept grasping for that and doing things to try to please people and doing things that just weren't being a productive husband, a good husband, a good man, and just trying to find anything to almost save myself in that time. I was chasing all these other things and they were all just empty. Not good for me, not good for my health and everything in general. There were a lot of things that needed to change in my life. It just got to a point where it was so heavy and everything seemed dark and like it was an end of a tunnel coming. And then eventually one night I opened up to Haley about a lot of things in my life and the things that I had not been truthful to her about."

Ty and Haley first met in the summer of 2007 when they were about 15 years old and their families were camping in motorhomes near the Charlotte Motor Speedway. A few years later, a long-distance relationship developed through all-night phone conversations while Haley was a student at Washington State University and Ty was racing and living near Charlotte. They married in 2014, and three years later their daughter,

Oakley, was born. But the couple was not prepared for the marital strife that loomed ahead.

"It was a very tough time for our marriage and our life in general," Ty recalls. "That was the first time I knew I couldn't do it anymore on my own. I had hit rock bottom and come to the end of myself." And that's when Ty asked God for help. He also started talking with Blake Koch, a Christian friend and fellow driver, about how his relationship with Christ gave him joy, purpose, and meaning. The couple sought marital counseling from Ray Wright, who had officiated their wedding and also worked for Richard Childress Racing as strength and conditioning coach. "He just scooped us up right away. He led me to getting my first Bible and pointed me in a direction to healing for ourselves from everything that was going on."

Then a family tragedy struck in early September 2018, when Haley's aunt and cousin were killed in a motorhome accident. Her uncle and several other cousins survived their injuries. Ty and Haley went to Washington state to grieve with her family. While there, they visited a church in the nearby city of Kirkland that Ty had discovered online while listening to sermons on YouTube. During a weekday visit to the megachurch, they stopped at a coffee shop on campus, and surprisingly Ty was recognized by the barista, who was a fan of his NASCAR team. The Pacific Northwest was not exactly NASCAR country, so Ty and Haley were taken aback by the quick connection they made at the church.

When they returned the following Sunday, the Dillons had never been more at odds. "That Sunday, we decided to go into the service, and we were at a breaking point almost in our marriage at that point in time," Haley says. "We didn't even sit next to each other that day at church. We were at such a brutal point in our marriage. We were just so broken and lost." But at the end of the worship service, unbeknownst to each other, Ty and Haley both raised their hands to repent of their sin, receive God's forgiveness, and publicly profess their faith in Jesus Christ. After receiving God's forgiveness and unconditional love, they were finally ready to start extending that same grace and forgiveness to each other. "It was us deciding that day that we are in," Haley says. "If you keep God at the center of your marriage, and you never give up on each other, it's always worth staying together. It's always worth working it out. Three strands are not easily broken. Every day, God's grace is new for our lives."

When Ty and Haley returned home to North Carolina, they began weekly online video meetings to study the Bible with a couple they had met at the church in Kirkland. "We were so quick to just open up because we wanted help and we wanted healing," Ty says. "We wanted to know how God can help us through this. We did Christian marriage counseling for a long time. It was the best thing and it still is and there's so many things that we've learned. Jesus has just completely changed our lives. We believed in Him, but now we know Him and love Him." And while Ty and Haley continued to grow in their understanding of God's Word, life's challenges kept coming.

In late 2020, Haley had a miscarriage during her 11th week of pregnancy. And the next year, Ty was without a full-time ride in the Cup Series. He says, "2021 was one of our best times of enjoying life and feeling so connected to God because we were vulnerable. We didn't know what was going to happen. I ended up racing about 16 times that year instead of the 38-race schedule. I think I ran all three series for four or five different teams, a couple different manufacturers. Just random, I would get a call. 'Hey, here's an opportunity.' We went from making a lot of money racing to losing money, actually, in a year. Looking at our life since becoming Christians, I think things have actually probably from the outside gotten even harder. But because Jesus is so important to our life, it hasn't pained us worse. If anything, year after year we find more growth and understanding in our relationship with Him, and He takes us to these deeper waters with Him and takes us even further every year. We've learned great empathy for each other. And in doing that, you start to learn how to do that in your workplace. You start to learn how to do that with other people in your life."

Over his 238 career starts in NASCAR, Ty has driven for a number of teams, including RCR Enterprises, Stewart-Haas Racing, Leavine Family Racing, Germain Racing, Petty GMS Racing, and Spire Motorsports. But for the native of Lewisville, North Carolina, his first Cup Series victory remains elusive. In 2024, he returned to racing full-time in the Craftsman Truck Series, driving the No. 25 Chevy Silverado with Rackley W.A.R. Now a father of three, Ty says, "This is about four years in a row of not really knowing what's next, but it's like God hasn't left us in this journey. He hasn't taken it away from us. So, He obviously has something here even though it's been up and down. When God's will takes place and you stay patient and are obedient to that, the reward is getting to see how it plays out in your life. And the rewards that come from that are so much deeper than you could have imagined."

21

Justin Allgaier

Chasing the Miraculous

IN HIS 14-PLUS SEASONS driving in NASCAR's Xfinity Series, Justin Allgaier has been the model of excellence and consistency. Justin's 2024 campaign marks his ninth season with JR Motorsports, making him their longest tenured and winningest driver. The Riverton, Illinois native was runner-up in the 2023 Xfinity Series points standings, winning four races and posting 15 top fives and 20 top tens on the way to his sixth appearance in the Championship 4. This marked the fourth time in six seasons that Justin won at least three times. His four victories also pushed him to 23 career wins, 20 of which have occurred in JR Motorsports Chevrolets.

Yet for all of Justin's success on the track, he says it's the relationships that he values more than trophies and records.

"I think for me, racecars are racecars, or chunks of metal for that matter without the people who are around it. And I think that's what's most important. For me, racing is just to succeed with people and the racing side of things will kind of come as they will." And if you're wondering what the people think about Justin, he has been voted Most Popular Driver in the Xfinity Series in 2019, 2020, 2021, and 2023. "My racing career is nothing short of miraculous," Justin says. "I think when you look at how things happened, there's been so many times that my racing career should have ended. And it didn't end. God put the right people or the right situations in front of me that has allowed me to succeed."

Growing up with Christian parents and a loving church family helped bend Justin's heart toward God early in life. "I'm blessed that I didn't go through a tumultuous path before professing my faith in Christ," he says. "I kind of grew up in the faith and fell in love with Jesus at an early age. And so, for me, I think that having that faith at a young age, getting baptized fairly early and being in the church really has made me put the emphasis on understanding my identity in Christ and understanding my purpose. I get to do what I love to do, and I have had success. But again, I think that for me, it's about relationships. I've been put in front of a ton of people, whether it be on TV or social media. My platform is very large. But I've also got a great opportunity each and every week to have 10 to 15 people who are in my inner circle that are on my race team who I can have those conversations with and I can help lead them to Christ. All we can do as stewards of God's Word is to give them our knowledge and to give them our love and understanding, and eventually God opens their eyes to what they are hearing, or they're willing to open their eyes to what God's telling them. I will never deny my faith or who I am as a person. And even if that becomes controversial at some point, I still will never ever waver from that."

At the age of 5, while most of his peers were into their coloring books, Justin was racing a quarter midget roadster. By age 12, he had already collected more than 100 wins and five championships. At 14, he was the youngest driver to compete in the A main race at the famous Chili Bowl. NASCAR Cup Series driver Kenny Schrader believed in Justin's potential so much that he donated an ARCA Series racecar to his family's race team. "It really kind of shaped the future of who I became and how things worked for me," Justin says. "His only requirement was we come to Charlotte and pick it up. I got to talk to Kenny about it and understand how the car works and functions and operates. We raced the ARCA Series, which is a way higher series than we could ever afford to possibly be a part of."

Justin raced part-time in the ARCA Series for three years, picking up a few sponsors along the way, before going full-time at age 20 and winning the championship two years later. While racing a full-time ARCA schedule on a shoestring budget, the Allgaiers were always looking to restock their thin inventory of parts and racecars. That is, until Justin's first-ever sponsor—who had donated $500 when Justin was only five years old—spent $100,000 to purchase 11 stock cars from a Cup Series team that was liquidating its assets. This included an inventory of parts worth $2 million as a free bonus for buying the entire fleet of racecars. Justin says, "At the time, the cheapest car we could find was like $50,000 apiece, and they wanted like right at $10,000 apiece for a car, and then they ended up giving us all these parts afterwards. It was miraculous that we even came close to have an opportunity to buy these cars."

But in the middle of Justin's 2008 ARCA championship season, he learned it would be the last for his family-owned team. "My dad came to me and said, 'We're out of money. My retirement is gone, your inheritance is gone. We spent every dime we can possibly spend. I don't know how to keep moving forward.' And so, you know, as a 22-year-old, I was kind of devastated because I felt like that was my last opportunity, especially because at that point 17-, 18-, 19-year-olds were all getting contracts to move up, and here I am already in my 20s."

Meanwhile, the first weekend of June, Justin was racing at Pocono Raceway in Pennsylvania and had a chance meeting with a representative of Team Penske. "I go out and I win the race that day," Justin says. "First time I'd ever won on a big track." The following week he was invited to a meeting with Team Penske reps in Charlotte. "I spent the last $700 I had in my bank account to buy a plane ticket to fly to Charlotte," Justin recalls. After a tour of the organization's 200,000-square-foot facility and a lunch interview, Justin headed back home to Illinois, his racing future still in doubt. Two weeks later, he received another invitation—this time for a Sunday meeting with Roger Penske in his motorhome near the IndyCar race at Chicagoland Speedway. Justin says, "He told me to give him 24 hours, and on Tuesday morning they sent a plane to pick me up. I flew to Detroit, Michigan. I sat in his hangar, and I signed my first NASCAR deal to drive for Roger Penske. So, I literally went from no opportunity to getting a full-time ride in NASCAR all within a matter of about two months."

Justin's ARCA championship, which included six wins, 14 top fives, and 16 top tens, had cemented a relationship with Roger Penske, who signed him to Penske Racing's developmental division. After a few races with Penske in 2008, Roger tapped Justin as the driver for his No. 12 Verizon Dodge. Now, at age 38, Justin is one of the senior drivers in a series that's largely considered the pathway to NASCAR's premier Cup Series.

But Justin has been there and done that too. In 2014 and 2015, he drove full-time in the Cup Series, piloting the No. 51 BRANDT Professional Agriculture Chevrolet for HScott Motorsports. "When I ran the Cup Series, I put a lot of pressure on myself," he says. "I kept trying to manage it on my own. I wanted to be able to control it. And the more I tried to control, the more out of control I got and spiraled. And I got to the point where I couldn't come home and leave the racing at the racetrack. I couldn't come home and be happy about what was going on. Here I am at the greatest point of my life. I just had my first child. I signed a Cup contract. All these things are going great, and I was just miserable."

Justin and his wife, Ashley, who began dating when they were 15 and got married at 19, agreed that their marriage and family was more important than racing in the Cup Series on Sundays. When Justin's two-year Cup Series contract expired at the end of 2015, his primary sponsor offered him a financial package for 2016 that just happened to match the exact dollar figure that JR Motorsports was seeking to sponsor one of their Xfinity Series race teams. Justin sensed God was giving him another opportunity. After all, prioritizing family and relationships is what had made Justin successful throughout his stock car racing career. "My wife and I, we shared a vehicle to do whatever we could just to make ends meet," he says. "And if it wasn't for my parents, there's no way we would have made it financially early in our marriage. They helped us buy some things that we would have never been able to buy. I know where my success isn't—it's not on earthly things."

Although there's a sense in which Justin still thinks he has some unfinished business in the Xfinity and Cup Series, he has no regrets. "While I would love to have a championship and love to be the most successful racecar driver on planet Earth, I don't need that to succeed or to fulfill what I feel like my role is in all of this. I love what I do. And I'm blessed to do what I love to do every day, and I'm going to keep giving 100 percent. And if it goes any further, great. And if my crew were to be done tomorrow, I'm still super thankful and super appreciative of what I've been able to accomplish, and I wouldn't trade it for the world."

22

Austin Dickey

Over the Wall for God

FOR 16 YEARS, Austin Dickey has gone over the wall as a pit crew member for some of NASCAR's legendary drivers, including Hall of Famers Jeff Gordon and Jimmie Johnson. As a front tire changer, Austin makes sure the lug nut securely holds the tire in place. Before the Next Gen racecar came on the scene in 2022, each tire was secured by five lug nuts, but current models have only one. Now more than ever, a tire changer's precision (or lack thereof) can be the difference between his driver contending for the lead or an early exit to the garage. "You're talking about tenths of a second for your brain to realize how tight these things are," Austin explains. "But you can always hear and feel more. As a tire changer you're hearing and you're feeling the gun and the ratchet.

Sometimes you hear the lug nut wrenching, but you don't feel it tightening. When a tire changer just goes by what they hear, that's where you start getting into the trouble of loose wheels."

Austin's tire change illustration is a good analogy for his spiritual condition during his late teens and early 20s. Growing up in a Christian home, he had heard the truth of God's Word. But he didn't feel that it applied to him, and he rejected its power to securely set him on the right path. He says, "I was a fence rider. I played the part of a good Christian boy when I needed to play it to the moms and dads to take their daughters out on dates, and then I definitely played the part of the jerk. And so, coming into NASCAR, I'm just graduating high school at 18. And I'm traveling, there's beer, there's women, there's all these things to experience, and so I took it. I went headfirst. And so, when I got cut loose, I was living this crazy life. I was doing some drugs. I was drinking. I was partying. I was doing a whole bunch of stuff."

And then Austin met Rachel. "I was like, something's different about this girl that I need to figure out. So, I started talking to her and she had this glow that I've never seen before. Like, it was unreal. It wasn't the girl that pulled me there. It was this light that she had about her. It was the love that she was giving spoke to my heart." While they were dating, Rachel told Austin about her first love, Jesus. Within a few months she stopped dating Austin when she learned that his profession of faith was merely lip service while his lifestyle told another story. The breakup sent Austin into a tailspin for several months. In his desperation, he cried out to God one night while lying face down on the floor in his bedroom. "I wanted that love that I felt, that light," he says. "So, I gave my life to Christ that night."

Austin had come to realize that his attraction to Rachel was much more than a physical attraction. He had seen Christ for the first time, and it was Rachel who embodied Jesus's love for him. "When she would come around me, it was gentle. It was honesty. It was love. I don't think I've ever truly felt loved like that by anybody else. She just truly showed unconditional love. Like a person should love a person the way Christ calls us to love a person. And that's what changed me. That's the light I saw, because no one's ever treated me like that before. And so that's what drew me in. God knows your heart language when He calls your name. And it's like the language that you know because He's calling you by name. And He knew me. And that's how He got my attention."

It took Austin about three months to summon up the courage to call Rachel and thank her for not just telling him but more importantly showing him what it means to have a new life in Christ. She agreed to meet him for a picnic lunch at a public park in Greensboro, North Carolina, about an hour from Austin's home in Concord. Austin's dad drove him to meet Rachel because his driver's license had been suspended after too many tickets for reckless driving and speeding. "I sat down with Rachel, and I apologized and asked her to forgive me. Soon thereafter, we went on another date. And six months later, we got engaged. And then a year later we got married."

After Austin became a Christian, his coworkers at Hendrick Motorsports were curious about the 180-degree change in his language, demeanor, temperament, and general disposition. He told them, "I promise, that's not me living now. It is definitely Christ in me. He's changed my life."

Another unmistakable difference in Austin's life is his insatiable appetite for God's Word. "I enjoy calming myself before the storm by reading Scripture, so I will read my Bible during the race," he says. "I like hearing God's Word tell me my value and what Christ has done for me before I go into that race. It's super calming. So, I know that my job isn't just my job and my worth isn't just in changing tires. When you start understanding your value, it kind of takes away the pressure in those moments of chaos."

About six years into their marriage, Austin and Rachel faced their biggest test of faith when she had a miscarriage at 20 weeks into her pregnancy. The couple had two young sons and were looking forward to welcoming a third child into their family when tragedy struck. "I got super angry with God," Austin says. "I felt like God told me 'Listen, all these things are mine. Nothing is because of you. It's all because of me.' But it was really humbling to hear God claiming that He owns me, and all things are created for His good and all things are done for His good. And so, when we first lost our unborn son, it took me about a week to really hear God's voice saying that, even though this is painful, He is with us and He will heal our hearts when we trust and obey Him when He says, 'Give Me your heart. Give Me your patience. Dive into Me. Lean further into Me and you'll be more comforted.'" Austin says that God also led Rachel to write a book about her suffering and what her heavenly Father taught her through her grief. "Our faith has grown immensely through our third son's death, who we named Asher," Austin says. "You start realizing God is there in the storm and calming it down because He's always going to take care of you. He's going to take care of the birds and the flowers and the bees and everything else around you. Why wouldn't He take care of you more? Why wouldn't He be the one to say, 'Listen, I got it.'"

After spending 14 years with Hendrick Motorsports, the 2024 season marked Austin's second as the front tire changer with 23XI Racing and Bubba Wallace's No. 23 Toyota. But Austin says his pit crew job title is not his primary mission in life. For that, he quotes 1 Peter 3:15: "But in your hearts honor Christ the Lord as holy, always being prepared to make a defense to anyone who asks you for a reason for the hope that is in you; yet do it with gentleness and respect."

Austin says, "My job is actually to share the gospel, since that's what God calls us to do. God is calling me right now to be a tire changer and to use that platform for Him because there's so many opportunities. People want to hear anything you have to say. It's where God starts using His words and helping me to know the Scriptures to be able to speak into people's lives, so the Holy Spirit may turn their hearts and soften them to know the love and the truth that God has for them. One of my spiritual gifts is to encourage, and so I'm very straight to the point. The Holy Spirit uses me a lot to help convict, but in a loving way. So, a lot of my buddies, who I'm really close with now, when we first met, they saw that I'm a Christian and I live by different standards than most, and they are drawn to that through the light of Christ in me. The standard is given in Scripture. And as iron sharpens iron, we're going to continue to grow in that."

23

Marty Snider

When You're Told You're Not Good Enough

DURING HIS 25-PLUS YEARS as a NASCAR reporter and host for NBC, Marty Snider has covered the sport literally from start to finish. As the host of the television network's prerace and postrace coverage, Marty also reports from pit road during Cup Series races. Having grown up around stock car racing, the High Point, North Carolina native has found a home in the world of motorsports. But Marty's journey to becoming an Emmy Award–winning sports broadcaster has been full of unexpected twists and turns.

"My father passed away, right in front of me," he says. "And that was a tough moment for me as a young boy, obviously. As you can imagine, any nine-year-old would struggle with their dad passing away very unexpectedly." Marty's father had suffered from rheumatic fever as a child, and it damaged his heart. Eventually, in the mid-1970s, he became one of the first heart patients to receive a pacemaker to help his heart function properly. "The pacemaker just quit one day," Marty recalls. "He had a heart attack right in front of me. And that was a tough time. You're questioning a lot as a young man. You're wondering what's happened. And I think there's a natural tendency to be mad at God and question that and not understand why your father was taken from you. I think I spent awhile in that process. I couldn't say I was mad at something. I didn't know what I was mad at. As a kid, I never rebelled or anything."

About a year before his dad's sudden death, Marty had acknowledged God as his heavenly Father and professed Jesus Christ as his Savior and Lord. And after his dad passed away, he continued attending church with his neighborhood friends and stayed connected with his church youth group. Throughout his childhood, Marty's spiritual formation was shaped by Bible teachers and mentors in his church.

Meanwhile, his stock car racing lineage was undeniable. "My family was in racing," he says. "My dad owned what is now considered a Cup Series team way back in the day. In the 1950s, it was just people racing back then. It wasn't a NASCAR team as you see it now. And so, I was always around it. My cousin drove. Jay Hedgecock was his name, and I would always hang out at his house and be around him. And then our family had a race team, and so we had a lot of people work for us over the years. Bobby Labonte's first job was with us, and Jeff Burton, who I now work with in television, one of his first jobs was with us." Even Kyle Petty could be found hanging around the race shop in High Point whenever he could get loose from his family's Petty Enterprises operation.

While the NASCAR influences from Marty's youth would serve him well for decades to come, during his high school and college years he was more fascinated by the idea of becoming a television sports broadcaster. He majored in political science at UNC Charlotte after not getting accepted at the University of North Carolina at Chapel Hill where he wanted to major in broadcast journalism. "My whole thing was I wanted to be in television," Marty says. His best friend's dad, Fred Blackman, a longtime TV news anchor for a local ABC affiliate station, recommended Marty for an internship in the sports department at Channel 8 WGHP. But after the internship, Marty's big break was a bust. "The guy who ran the sports department told me I never would be good enough to be on live television and said, 'So we're not going to give you a job.'"

Undeterred, Marty discovered a job opportunity at an NBC affiliate in Greenville, South Carolina, and drove from Greensboro to personally deliver his résumé and videotape of short broadcast clips. To his surprise, he got the job and Marty's television broadcast career was launched in 1994. "I don't know how, but the Lord was looking after me on that one for sure," he says. "And so, I worked there for a while, and I started doing live shots talking about racing for other NBC affiliates. They all kept asking for me to keep doing them because I knew about racing."

Growing up in the world of motorsports had provided Marty insights about NASCAR that distinguished him among his broadcast peers. "They kind of do it because they have to and it's in their market, and they cover it once a year, and then they forget about it. Well, I was already all up in it, knew a lot of people in the sport and always understood it. So, I made the very rare jump from a local affiliate to ESPN when ESPN was starting a new show called *NASCAR Today*." While at ESPN, Marty got experience in front of the camera as well as producing behind the camera. He recalls, "The producer of the live races at the time told me the same thing as the guy who told me 'you'll never be good enough to be on live television.' And I just took it as motivation."

A stint with Motor Racing Network radio led to television job opportunities with Turner Sports and CNN. "And then Turner and NBC got the NASCAR package together, and I've been at NBC ever since 1999," he says. "It's kind of crazy to think of how blessed I've been to be able to stay in one place. It doesn't happen in network television very much, but I've got great bosses and they have put me in a good spot to stay there for a long time." When Marty's not covering NASCAR or the IndyCar Series, he has covered the NFL, the NBA, and the NCAA men's college basketball tournament. Other NBC Sports assignments have taken him to the 2008 Beijing Olympics, professional bull riding competitions, off-road racing, and open-wheel racing. Marty says, "It's pretty full-time around the year for me. God has been very generous to me on the career front, to have a great career with NBC and to have had the run that we have." Marty coproduced HBO's Emmy-winning series *24/7*, featuring NASCAR Hall of Fame inductee Jimmie Johnson. He also cohosted *The Morning Drive* on SiriusXM's NASCAR channel, and he has been recognized with several awards throughout his broadcasting career, including six network Emmys and NASCAR.com's 2007 Pit Reporter of the Year.

As a testament to God's faithfulness in his life despite his father's untimely death, Marty quotes Jeremiah 29:11: "For I know the plans I have for you, declares the LORD, plans for welfare and not for evil, to give you a future and a hope." He says that throughout his life and career he has prayed that God would open and close doors of opportunity according to His will. "You don't ever imagine that you're going to have a 25-year network career and win Emmys for what you do. We've been able to do so much because of that career, but it's also blessed us that we can bless others as well."

From launching a national fraternity during his college days to helping start a new church and participating regularly in a men's Bible study group, Marty says that his personal relationship with Jesus has compelled and inspired him throughout his life to strive to be a servant leader. "For me, that's been a core tenet of who I am and how I operate. I try to take that first hour of my day to spend time with the Lord and just pray, 'Show me where You're working, show me what You want me to be doing.' It's not always easy. It's certainly a weekly goal."

Of all Marty's career accomplishments, he's most grateful for more than three decades of marriage to his wife, Andrea, and for their two sons and daughter. "Our kids know the Lord, and that's the biggest part that makes me proud as a parent," he says. As for his NASCAR roots, they keep spreading: his oldest son, Myatt, won his first Xfinity Series race at Homestead-Miami Speedway in February 2021. And while the joys of fatherhood sometimes remind Marty of what might have been if his dad had lived, he refuses to be regretful. "I know that the Lord was working in all of that, and all things work for His good. I think my dad's death certainly changed my life in a lot of bad ways. But at the end of the day, in a lot of good ways as well."

24

Jason Ratcliff

The Ultimate Crew Chief

AS A NASCAR CREW CHIEF who has spent 24 years across both the Xfinity and Cup Series, Jason Ratcliff has teamed up with some of the sport's winningest drivers of the 21st century, including Matt Kenseth, Kyle Busch, Joey Logano, Tony Stewart, and Denny Hamlin. His 801 starts atop the pit box have yielded 72 victories—15 in the Cup Series and a record-high 57 wins in the Xfinity Series. During Jason's career as a crew chief with Joe Gibbs Racing, his teams' combined efforts have earned them 49 pole positions and 406 top-ten finishes—an astounding 50.7 percent of their races. Of those, 239 were top fives.

In 2024, after 18 years with JGR, Jason took on a new role as the team/driver coordinator for the organization's Xfinity and ARCA Menards Series programs. Now in his late 50s, the Sumter, South Carolina native is all about mentoring the next generation of NASCAR drivers and crew chiefs. His lifetime of experience includes lessons learned from both success and failure. "I'm excited to transition into this new role with Joe Gibbs Racing," he says. "The team has become home to me over the years, and I'm grateful that they have grown with me as my career has evolved. The opportunity to help the next generation of crew chiefs and drivers is something that means a lot to me and it means the world that I get to do it at the same team that I have built my legacy with."[1]

Jason started developing his mechanical skills at age 10. His father, George, was a nondenominational minister who also bought and sold cars to help support his family. Jason would help his dad replace water pumps and belts on the used vehicles before reselling them. Throughout his teen-age years, Jason enjoyed hot-rodding and helping local short-track racers work on their cars. When his father's ministry led the family to move to Louisiana and Texas, Jason quickly acclimated himself to the local racing community. And of course, he attended church regularly. Jason says, "My dad was a minister, and I may not have wanted to have been in church every Sunday morning and Sunday night, but I was there, which is good in retrospect. I look back at that as such a benefit, what a blessing. I gave my life to the Lord when I was 12, but I don't know that I fully surrendered and trusted Him until later in life. And thankfully, God was patient and allowed that opportunity for me."

After working with local sprint car teams, Jason aspired to a full-time career in stock car racing. He got his first job in NASCAR in 1995 as a mechanic and rear tire changer for Sadler Brothers Racing based in Nashville, Tennessee. In 2000, after five years as a mechanic and tire changer with various teams, he landed his first crew chief opportunity with Brewco Motorsports in what's now the Xfinity Series. Victories came early with driver Jamie McMurray and former series champ David Green before Jason landed with Joe Gibbs Racing in 2005.

Three years later, Jason teamed up with Kyle Busch to dominate the Xfinity Series by winning 33 races between 2008 and 2011, including the 2009 series title. During that championship campaign, Busch led the season's races for an impressive 41 percent of the total laps.[2] Then, as a crew chief in the Cup Series, Jason teamed up with Matt Kenseth to win seven races in 2013 and finish runner-up in the season point standings. The duo made multiple playoff appearances over the next four seasons. Jason returned to the Xfinity Series in 2018, where he continued his winning ways with several different young drivers. In 2023, Jason guided Ty Gibbs and Ryan Truex to victory lane as well as veteran Denny Hamlin.

Communication is key, Jason says, when working with multiple drivers who have different personalities. For example, a car driving tight to one driver might feel loose to another. Keeping the mechanics, engineers, pit crew members, and drivers on the same page and moving in the same direction from week to week requires a lot of attention to detail. Steve deSouza, executive vice president of JGR's Xfinity and ARCA programs, says Jason is uniquely equipped for his role: "He is a true professional and offers a veteran mindset that a lot of our younger crew chiefs and drivers could benefit immensely from. When you consider his attention to detail, proven success, and consistent composure, it's clear that this new role suits him. As we look ahead to 2024, we are grateful to have him as a leader and role model for all the growing talent that we have within our organization."[3]

Being a role model, Jason says, requires that he allow God to be his ultimate crew chief. "First and foremost, He gave me a book, the Bible, that is great for instruction. So that's His word. That's how He directs me." But he admits that God's Word didn't always take precedence in his life. "As humans, it's easy to make our careers a form of an idol because it brings value to us. We think that's where purpose comes from and you think that you're going to be completely happy and fulfilled when you reach that next thing that you're after. Like 'If I could just win 10 races. If I could just win a championship, this is going to be the greatest thing, and it's going to be my ultimate fulfillment in life.' And you win that first championship and then it's like 'I really just need to win three. It's not what I thought it was going be like.' I reached the pinnacle and it was great for a moment, but it didn't last."

Now, Jason says, instead of "eating, breathing, drinking, and sleeping" his job, "every day, I wake up and open the Word of God and there's going to be something there that just draws me closer to God. No matter where I'm at, no matter what I'm doing, I can stop and have that direct line of communication. And my growth tomorrow will always be one step closer than today. I think that's one degree of glory to the next."

As a crew chief, Jason says, he would often defer to the spotter who could view the entire race unfolding from high above the grandstand. "And then obviously, when we talk about the spotter from a spiritual standpoint, the Holy Spirit is the Spotter. He's the One who is communicating all the time, relaying information, convicting, encouraging, witnessing, whatever that looks like."

Over the years, Jason has led Bible studies with his team, but he often employs a less direct approach. He says, "My door is always open. They know where I stand. I want their ears to be open and their hearts to be open."

25

Chris Rice

Blessed to Be a Blessing

WHEN CHRIS RICE WAS HIRED as general manager and crew chief of Kaulig Racing on October 31, 2015, the organization's Xfinity Series debut at Daytona International Speedway was barely three-and-a-half months away. Starting with literally nothing but the owner's funding, Chris was tasked with assembling the race team. That meant finding a race shop, stock cars, and equipment, as well as recruiting a driver, mechanics, pit crew, and support personnel. An opportunity some might have considered a nightmare Chris embraced as a dream come true.

The fledgling race team qualified to start in ninth position for their inaugural race. And when the checkered flag dropped and the smoke from the winner's burnout cleared, Blake Koch had piloted the No. 11 Chevrolet Camaro to a ninth-place finish—the same position he started from. Remarkably, by the end of that first season, Kaulig Racing had qualified for the playoffs, and they repeated as playoff contenders in their second and third seasons.

As a result of Kaulig's quick start in the Xfinity Series, Chris was named president of the company in 2018. The organization has grown to field six cars—four in Xfinity and two in the Cup Series. With more than 20 wins in the Xfinity Series, Kaulig achieved another huge milestone in 2021 by capturing its first Cup Series victory when AJ Allmendinger won the road course race at the prestigious Indianapolis Motor Speedway. AJ captured the team's second Cup Series victory at the Charlotte ROVAL in 2023, another road course victory.

Chris's fast start in launching a new NASCAR team was actually years in the making. Growing up in South Boston, Virginia, stock car racing was a way of life for the Rice family. From about age 10, Chris worked alongside his father and uncle while they built late model stock cars. Through the mid- to late-1980s, Chris was a member of Jeff Burton's late model team. At 15 years old, Chris worked as the gasman on Burton's pit crew when they raced at South Boston Speedway, which was managed by Chris's mother, Cathy. When Burton first competed part-time in the Busch Grand National Series, now known as the Xfinity Series, Chris's dad was his crew chief and Chris was his gasman.

During high school, Chris worked as a mechanic and spotter for Sadler Motorsports when Hermie Sadler was driving part-time in the Busch Grand National Series. After graduating in 1992, Chris went to work full-time on Hermie's team while also working on his associate's degree in college. Hermie was named Rookie of the Year in 1993 as a full-time driver in the Busch Series, and the next year Chris got his first experience as a crew chief for Hermie's younger brother, Elliott Sadler, who was competing in the late model stock car division. After winning their first race together at Ace Speedway in Altamahaw, North Carolina, in 1994, the duo clinched a championship the following season at South Boston Speedway, Chris's hometown racetrack. Chris continued working as crew chief in the late model stock car division through the 1990s while also racing late model trucks for his father's team.

Chris's breakthrough with Petty Enterprises came in 2001 when he was hired with driver Buckshot Jones, for whom he had worked as shock specialist and spotter. Following a brief stint with Bill Davis Racing, in 2003 Chris got his first opportunity as a crew chief in the Busch Series with driver Scott Wimmer. Over the next decade, he was a crew chief for RAB Racing and NTS Motorsports before finally joining Kaulig Racing.

Growing up in the world of stock car racing and competing at every level along his way to the pinnacle of NASCAR's premier racing series, Chris has been a part of nearly every face of a race team. You might think that his wealth of experience seems heavy at the top of an organization's chain of command, but that's not how Chris operates. He says, "Nobody works for me. We work together."

A few years ago, Chris realized that he needed some help. His "whatever it takes" mentality to build and launch an extremely competitive NASCAR team had taken a toll on his physical health. While being there for everyone else in the company, Chris's weight had ballooned to nearly 300 pounds and he couldn't do a single push-up. In early 2022, his wife,

Tammy, helped him cut nearly all sugar out of his diet for two months. Then he started working out with Tammy at the gym as well as doing CrossFit with a trainer. Always the selfless encourager and motivator, Chris regularly shared his weight-loss and fitness journey on social media, including posting videos of his 5:30 a.m. workouts and celebrating milestones like his 260-pound back squat. Over the course of several months, Chris lost more than 50 pounds and inspired three of his Xfinity crew chiefs to lose a combined 121 pounds.

Life on the road for a NASCAR team is one of the most grueling in professional sports. The season starts in February and runs through November. There are 33 weeks in the Xfinity Series schedule and nearly 40 weeks in the Cup Series, including exhibition events and 36 races for the championship standings. Chris is on the road for the full schedule, so to stay healthy and energized, his race day ritual on Saturdays usually includes a two-mile run and several sets of sit-ups and push-ups. Tammy, who also reached her weight-loss goal, often helps keep Chris's eating on track during race weekends by packing bags for him filled with protein and energy bars and food that fits their meal plan. And not only has Tammy been her husband's accountability partner health-wise, she's also impacted him spiritually during their 25-year marriage. Early in their marriage, Tammy attended church without Chris. She was a Christian at the time, but he wasn't. "She was praying for me every single day," Chris says. Then, shortly after their second daughter was born, he realized that he needed to commit his life to Christ so that he could be a Christian example for his daughters and encourage them to have a personal relationship with Jesus too. "I wanted to see my kids have that," he says.

Chris and Tammy are grateful for God's blessings on their lives spiritually and financially. They both grew up with very little materially and struggled to make ends meet early in their marriage. "We spent our first little bit with very little," Chris says. "No money, no nothing, not knowing how we were going to make it to the next paycheck." That's why they enjoy giving back to the community. "Being on the NASCAR Foundation Board of Directors is very special because you get to be a part of things that are bigger than racing. We love the competition side of what we do, but it is truly an honor to be on a decision-making team when it comes to improving the lives of children through the NASCAR community."[1]

"I've always been that guy who has tried to help the next person even if it hurts me," he says. For Chris, it's all about living life with a purpose. "You just got to take every moment like it's the last moment."

26

Jessica Fickenscher

A Heart to Serve

AS THE CHIEF EXPERIENCE OFFICER for Speedway Motorsports, LLC, Jessica Fickenscher is passionate about helping ensure that motorsports fans have a great time whether their favorite driver wins or not. "Anything that the fan touches, I'm involved with in some form or fashion," Jessica says. From the fan's ticket-buying experience to their engagement with a venue's ushers and ticket takers to their interaction with food, beverage, and merchandise operations—it all matters to Jessica.

Now multiply those expectations across the company's 11 racing venues—Atlanta Motor Speedway, Bristol Motor Speedway, Charlotte Motor Speedway, Dover Motor Speedway, Kentucky Speedway, Las Vegas Motor Speedway, Nashville Superspeedway, New Hampshire Motor Speedway, North Wilkesboro Speedway, Sonoma Raceway, and Texas Motor Speedway—and you can see that Jessica's job responsibilities are great. But that's not all. As managing director of Speedway Children's Charities, Jessica has helped raise tens of millions of dollars for those in need. And, by the way, she also oversees the US Legend Cars program for youngsters who dream of racing in NASCAR when they come of age.

Jessica says that during her 28-year career with Speedway Motorsports, she's been blessed to be a part of some amazingly fulfilling projects. But she admits that one assignment seemed nearly impossible when the idea was initially suggested. "Taking a racetrack that had been sitting dormant for nearly 30 years and bringing it back?" Jessica asks rhetorically. "If you would have suggested that to me five years ago, I would have said, 'You're crazy!'" But as executive director for the 2023 NASCAR All-Star Race at North Wilkesboro Speedway, Jessica witnessed the impossible become a reality—and in only eight months. "There's been some amazing things I've gotten to do, but this is definitely number one on the list."

Hosting the NASCAR All-Star Race at North Wilkesboro Speedway marked a doubly iconic moment for the sport's 75th anniversary—a tribute to the past and a vision for the future. The last time the green flag had dropped to start a Cup race on the 0.625-mile oval in Wilkes County, North Carolina, was September 29, 1996, when Jeff Gordon captured the checkered flag at the Tyson Holly Farms 400. In the nearly three decades since then, NASCAR had expanded its footprint nationwide, adding racing venues to the schedule that stretched from the East Coast to the West Coast. However, as NASCAR's popularity gained momentum across the country, time seemingly ran out for some of the more historic racetracks like the one at North Wilkesboro, which had opened in 1949 in the foothills of the Blue Ridge Mountains just 80 miles north of Charlotte, the stock car capital.

But when NASCAR Hall of Fame legend Dale Earnhardt Jr. and Speedway Motorsports president and CEO Marcus Smith began casting the vision for a racetrack resurrection, things started to happen. Before long, local volunteers descended on North Wilkesboro to take back the dilapidated track from the wild. Over five cold days in January 2021, volunteers cleared all the weeds and brush that had overgrown the venue while it lay dormant for decades. The track was then digitally scanned for use in a subscription-based eNASCAR iRacing event, an online racing simulation video game. "Dale Jr. never let up on the gas with Marcus in trying to bring that track back," Jessica says. In November 2021, the North Carolina legislature allocated $18 million from federal COVID-19 relief funding that the state had received for economic revitalization to put the racetrack back in business. And on August 31, 2022, 15,000 fans were in the stands to watch Dale Earnhardt Jr. compete in a late model stock car race, even while the venue had to bring in portable restroom units because the plumbing was still in such disrepair.

Jessica says that the opportunity to collaborate with "the best of the best" from Speedway Motorsports management teams across the country, many of whom she has known and worked with for more than 20 years, made planning, coordinating, and implementing the renovation of North Wilkesboro Speedway extremely gratifying. Beyond restoring and updating the venue's structural, electrical, and plumbing systems, Jessica's biggest concern was anticipating and addressing the traffic and parking challenges that always arise with opening a new racing venue. For that, she solicited the help of traffic and parking experts both locally and from around the country. Jessica also prayed every morning, asking God for wisdom and discernment to lead her team and make the most strategic and effective decisions for the project's success. "It's easy when you're in a leadership role to think that you're in control of everything, but you're not," she says. "There's only one person in control of everything and you got to remember that's God. Ground yourself and center yourself on that truth."

When the 2023 All-Star Race was over and all 25,000 fans hailing from 50 states and eight countries had exited the premises, Jessica's biggest concerns had been averted. She says, "God definitely answered my prayers. We had traffic cleared within one hour and 43 minutes." North Wilkesboro Speedway would again host the All-Star Race in May 2024. "Seeing everybody come together, and seeing everyone so proud of their community, it was really special. There was just an electricity in the air that I can't explain, and I've been to Super Bowls and Final Fours and never felt anything like that."

When Jessica started her career at Speedway Motorsports as a 19-year-old intern from Belmont Abbey College, she says she had no idea what her degree in sports management and business administration would yield. "I was never the smartest, but I'll outwork anybody. When you love what you do, you put everything you've got into it. I couldn't imagine being at a job where we didn't end meetings in prayer. That's who we are. We don't shy away from that."

That selfless collaborative spirit that has made Jessica successful in her career is rooted in her faith that has guided her since she committed her life to Christ as a child. And as a wife and a mother of two sons, she relies on those same biblical convictions to serve her family, friends, and coworkers well. "I feel like you need your tribe to help you get through things," she says. "You can't get through things on your own. I think having a small Bible study group is really important. Trust God. Put all your trust in Him. If you're not looking to God to depend on Him to help you through situations and decisions, then I feel like you're lost."

27

Jordan Anderson

Embracing the Journey

TO SAY THAT JORDAN ANDERSON'S NASCAR career has been forged through fire would not be an overstatement. Video of Jordan's truck erupting in flames during the Craftsman Truck Series race at Talladega Superspeedway on October 1, 2022, looks like a movie trailer for a box office thriller, but it was all too real for the Forest Acres, South Carolina native.

Jordan had qualified ninth in the 36-truck field and was running fourth on Lap 19 when smoke started billowing from the truck as flames engulfed it. He drove off the banking between Turn 1 and Turn 2, then started sliding and slammed the brakes, which turned him back up the track as flames darted through the front wheel wells and the back of the vehicle. As Jordan battled to regain control of his rolling inferno, the field of trucks swerved by him. Before hitting the SAFER barrier head-on along the inside wall, Jordan removed his seat belts, disconnected the steering wheel, and lowered the window net. As his truck hit the wall, the impact helped Jordan thrust himself out the driver's side window. "I jumped out of that thing and landed right on top of the wall," he says. "Three or four seconds earlier and it would have probably been me in between that truck and the wall coming together.

"Everything was just like slow motion. I saw the fire. I started to feel the fire getting hotter and hotter. I shut the motor off. Usually when you have a fire in a racecar it gets hot and it quickly goes out, but this just kept getting hotter and hotter, and just kept intensifying, and it finally got to a point where I was like, 'I can't take this anymore. Whatever's on the outside of this moving truck is better than just sitting here taking this,' so that was when I dropped the window net and took the steering wheel off while still going 80 miles an hour."

Jordan estimates that when his truck hit the safety barrier, the vehicle was traveling about 30 miles per hour. As smoke gushed from the truck, he climbed atop the SAFER barrier along the inside wall and jumped down and laid flat on his back as safety crew members arrived. Jordan was airlifted by helicopter to a local hospital where he was treated for second- and third-degree burns on his arms and legs. He says the flames burned about 20 percent of his body, including his eyelashes, cheeks, neck, right hand, right arm, and both knees. The heat was so intense that the front windshield started to crack as smoke enveloped the cockpit. "Looking back on it, I see how

God was definitely at work in that whole deal for me to get out of the truck while it was still moving." He says that during his recovery he also valued the extra time he had with Kendall, his wife of six months. "So, for us that was kind of a blessing. She and I were able to spend three weeks together."

Jordan was making his 138th Camping World Truck Series start that October day at Talladega. After qualifying to start the race near the front of the pack in the top 10, he liked his chances on the 2.66-mile oval superspeedway. And why not? He was driving the same truck that had garnered him back-to-back second-place finishes in the 100-lap Truck Series season openers at Daytona International Speedway the previous two years. Following his second-place finish there in 2020, Jordan said in a postrace interview, "This finish tonight, hopefully, is for every underdog in America, every kid that stays up late and works on his dirt late model or his Legends car and dreams of coming here to Daytona. Hopefully, this finish tonight encourages them to never give up on their dreams."[1] That runner-up finish was a career best for him. And he matched it in the 2021 season opener at Daytona. Jordan says, "Finishing second the following year was even crazier, you know, to be that close again. But if you go back and watch that interview that I gave after the race, I mean, I just have always felt like it was an honor to be here."

But eventually the superspeedway racing took its toll on the truck that Jordan had rebuilt in the winter of 2019. "The truck that finished second those two years back-to-back was the same one that caught on fire," he says. "When I bought that truck over that winter, it didn't have a body on it. It was missing some parts and pieces. And so, I spent a lot of money on it. And we built it and sunk a lot of time and effort into it.

We were going all in on this one. That was kind of the way we looked at that."

Frankly, Jordan has been all in on the stock car racing journey since he started racing go-karts at age 7, just a year after he professed his faith in Jesus Christ as his Savior and Lord. "My Christian faith and racing have really been hand in hand over the years," he says. "I've been through a lot of ups and downs to make this work, and quitting and giving up has never been an option. I think that, as a Christian, God has kind of instilled in my DNA a no-quit mindset. Similarly, when you look through so many of the accounts in the Bible, God's people probably had no business fighting, but because of their faith in God and His strength, that's the way things went."

After competing in the Truck Series from 2014 through 2017, Jordan sensed God leading him to take a step of faith and start his own motorsports company in 2018. "I started the team just to help give myself an opportunity to go race," he says. He had earned a business management degree from Belmont Abbey College and was ready to put it to work to help solicit business partnerships and sponsorships to fund his racing team. He had been cheated once by a race team owner in 2014 who had written about $50,000 in bad checks, much of which Jordan had to cover by selling his personal racecars and equipment.

Jordan started developing his entrepreneurial skills as a child while seeking sponsorships for his racing endeavors. When he was 12 years old, he offered the owner of a car dealership the advertising rights to the hood of his racecar. "I've got my three-ring binder put together with magazine clippings and pictures of our racecar, and I asked for $5,000 to be on the hood of my bandolero car," Jordan recalls. "He brings me back up there and sits me in his chair and he goes, 'I'm going to teach you a little life lesson here, Jordan. You've undervalued the value of your racing program and what you're worth. Here's a check for $10,000 to sponsor your racecar. And I want to teach you to never settle for less and always go for more and don't ever undersell yourself.'"

Jordan has also learned how to maximize his equipment. He drove one truck an entire season and often drove the dually that trailered his ride. "Most people don't realize how razor sharp of an edge that a lot of race teams operate on from week to week to make it sustainable and survive," he says. "And there's a lot of blood, sweat, and tears that has gone into this team from day one. But even up until a year or two ago, how close things were to the brink of the team shutting down just from not having enough funds. So, fighting through that was one of those business decisions there." And Jordan says that he's learned a lot of spiritual lessons through owning his own race team. "It's kind of like iron sharpens iron. So, sometimes, through pain and through those tough times is the way that God tests our faith and makes us stronger through those situations that can be trying, but they make us stronger as a result of it."

In the winter of 2022, Jordan sold 80 percent of his truck inventory to fund a second Chevrolet Camaro in the Xfinity Series. Jordan Anderson Racing Bommarito Autosport competed for the 2023 season with Rookie of the Year contender Parker Retzlaff driving the No. 31 car, while playoff contender Jeb Burton drove the No. 27 car. Burton collected JAR's first Xfinity Series victory in April 2023 at the Ag-Pro 300 at Talladega—the same superspeedway where six months earlier Jordan had his fiery crash. "For that to be our team's first win was crazy, when you consider that the last time I left from there was in a helicopter for emergency medical treatment following my accident," he says.

In August 2023, Jordan's race team reached another milestone when he raced for the first time since the accident, competing in an Xfinity Series race at Daytona with his other two team-owned cars. "My father-in-law, Larry McReynolds, got to crew chief for me, and we ended up finishing 15th that night," he says. "That for me kind of answered a lot of questions. I still want to do this. I still can do this. This is something I've dreamed about my whole life. To have the opportunity to be involved in it is pretty special. And that's the fuel that keeps me pushing through the long days. Seeing this thing grow and take off is pretty crazy, and I've still got plenty that I want to accomplish behind the wheel. That's not over by any means. It's just that the ownership side has taken a bigger role for now. On the ownership side, this is something I hope to do for the next 50 years and be here to create something that's going to be here long after I'm gone. So, it is exciting to see where this journey has taken us. Embracing the journey that we've been on has been a big motto that we've tried to live by, but it has been really cool to see what's all come of it."

Jordan credits his parents, Cliff and Sherry, for their unwavering support and encouragement to relentlessly pursue his NASCAR dream while honoring God every step of the way. He says, "My dad is the ultimate example of an amazing father and the importance of being true to your faith and being true to make time for God. We have such a great relationship. There's nothing that ever goes on that I don't talk to him about or ask his advice. One of my favorite Bible verses is Proverbs 3:5–6. God has got a plan for you through all things. It is amazing to look back on all those life events and see what God had planned through all that stuff. Lots of doors closed, and other doors have opened through that whole journey."

28

Phil Parsons

Persevering Through Prayer

GROWING UP IN DETROIT, MICHIGAN, Phil Parsons aspired to follow in his older brother's tracks. Benny Parsons, 16 years Phil's senior, had a head start on his stock car racing career and eventually arrived in the NASCAR Hall of Fame. By the time Phil was 12, Benny was gaining traction in the Cup Series with each victory on the track. Phil would spend summers in North Carolina helping with Benny's race team. "Every waking moment that I had off school or summertime or whatever, I always came down south to the races," Phil says. "My dad was a huge race fan. That's originally what led my brother into racing."

After graduating from high school, Phil dutifully attended college at the advice of his parents. But he couldn't find anything on campus that piqued his interest like the racetrack. "I didn't just want to race," he says. "I wanted to be the best ever. I wanted to be Richard Petty. I finally started racing while I was in college up in Michigan, but I raced primarily down south. I would leave school Friday, and me and a friend would drive to wherever the race might be, whether it's in North Carolina, Virginia, or Tennessee. Then turn around and drive back home and be back to school on Monday." After four years of college, Phil joined Benny's team while competing in NASCAR's feeder program, the Goody's Dash Series. "When I finally got out of school, my brother was racing for a team that was based in Savannah, Georgia," Phil says. "I moved down to Savannah for about six months, still racing while I was down there, and then made the move to North Carolina in December of 1979 to race in the late model sportsman division, which is kind of the forerunner of the Xfinity Series." Phil readily acknowledges that being Benny's younger brother helped him break into the sport. "There's no doubt it opened a number of doors for me that would not have been opened. I mean, nepotism is alive and well in motorsports."

When the Busch Grand National Series (now the Xfinity Series) launched in 1982, Phil was chosen by Johnny Hayes Racing to drive the No. 28 Pontiac. In the third race of the inaugural season, Phil finished ahead of David Pearson, one of his racing heroes, at Bristol Motor Speedway to claim his first victory at NASCAR's second highest level of racing. Not long thereafter, Phil partnered with a tobacco company as his lead sponsor for the Cup Series. During an appearance with teammate Harry Gant at the Lowe's store in North Wilkesboro, North Carolina, he met his future wife, Marcia, who worked with Lowe's promotional events. The couple married two years later.

In 1983, Phil made five Cup Series starts driving the No. 66 Skoal car. But more importantly, he became his brother's teammate, as Benny drove the No. 55 car for Hayes. Phil's 13th place finish in the Daytona 500 for his NASCAR debut made quite the first impression among fans and media alike. But the most memorable moment of that season came during Lap 72 of the Winston 500 when the rookie made contact with Darrell Waltrip, causing Phil's car to crash into the outside retaining wall, then flip wildly before coming to rest in a heap in the infield. The wreck, which is still considered one of the most spectacular crashes in the history of Talladega Superspeedway, resulted in a massive pileup as Phil's car barrel-rolled about a dozen times in the midst of traffic. The mayhem on the track upset Phil's big brother so deeply that Benny began screaming over the radio for a relief driver so he could get out of the car and go be with his younger brother.

Phil suffered a broken shoulder and was sidelined for six weeks as a result of that crash. But his NASCAR dream was still alive. He competed a majority of the schedule in 1984, garnering three top tens and a handful of other strong finishes. Equally important, being mindful of his team's limited resources, he kept the racecar in one piece on most occasions. Phil finished that season as runner-up to Rusty Wallace for Rookie of the Year.

The 1988 season would produce Phil's greatest career achievement—his first and only NASCAR Cup victory. The historic milestone came in the Winston 500 at Talladega Superspeedway, where he'd had his horrific crash five years earlier. After remaining on the track during an early caution flag and instead pitting under the green flag, Phil was able to stay on the lead lap and avoid being lapped by race leader Ken Schrader. Then, when Schrader lost control of his racecar, causing another caution flag, the remaining cars on the track had to reset. Phil raced to the front of the pack to lead 52 laps and score the victory by a car length over future Hall of Famer Bobby Allison. "It felt like I had worked towards that from the time I was five years old," Phil says. "And I was 30 years old when that happened. We had a really good year, and it started out really good with a third-place finish at the Daytona 500." At the end of the season, Phil ranked ninth in the championship points standings as the driver of the No. 55 Oldsmobile.

As memorable as Phil's win was at Talladega, the second race there later that season was unforgettable for all the wrong reasons. He was running in third place with about 10 laps to go when an explosion occurred inside the racecar. To his amazement, the interior of the car reached 125 degrees, which automatically triggered the fire extinguisher to activate. "I thought I blew an engine and so I shut the engine off and pulled over out of the way," Phil recalls. "Nobody even knew that they [extinguishers] were thermostatically controlled, not manually controlled. So, it took me out of contention. That was 1988 and I remember it like it was yesterday. And it's still hard to swallow today because I felt like I was in a great position to win again. But unfortunately, the rest of my career, I didn't have that many opportunities to win."

Then the unexpected happened in 1989. "I've been racing for eight or nine years, and that was the first time in my career that I had a year that wasn't as good as the year before," Phil says. "And that was tough. So, I felt like I needed to make a move to another team because I didn't feel like that was going to get any better. When I moved to another team in 1990, we raced three races and I got fired. I don't know where I go from here. I don't have a job. I've never not had a job. I don't know exactly what to do." But Phil did know Who to ask. "I prayed for guidance. I prayed that whatever the Lord wanted and wherever the Lord felt like I should be, that that door would open."

Phil had learned a lot about prayer over the years from his wife and her parents. He had also grown spiritually through his association with Motor Racing Outreach. Phil says, "We came in probably within five or six months from the time the Bible study group was formed, and then it kind of blossomed from there." NASCAR drivers Darrell Waltrip and Lake Speed helped launch the Bible study group with their wives, and Phil and Marcia joined soon thereafter. "I saw something in them as far as on Sundays being able to try to beat each other's brains out essentially on the racetrack, but then lived their lives with Christianity as their guiding force. We got to be very good friends with them even after our careers ended and to this day, and that's why I feel so fortunate to be involved with MRO and the people that are involved with MRO."

After much prayer, Phil and Marcia decided to move forward. "Marcia and I did a lot of soul-searching, and it was really her idea," he says. She suggested to Phil, "Why don't we get a racecar, and then we'll race when we can afford it or when we get sponsorship?" For the next several years, Phil raced primarily in the second-tier Busch Series. "We did win a race in Charlotte, and in our own car back in 1994, which was pretty spectacular, really." And just like his late brother, Benny, who became a NASCAR television analyst after retiring from his racing career, Phil also segued from the cockpit to the announcer's booth. After competing in the Cup Series from 1983 to 1998 and the Xfinity Series from 1982 to 2000, he became an analyst for ESPN's coverage of the Truck Series. "So basically, I quit driving after the 2000 season and started doing television, and I've been doing TV ever since."

29

Ryan Dextraze

The Power of Forgiveness

AS A FRONT SUSPENSION MECHANIC for Legacy Motor Club, Ryan Dextraze's primary responsibility is to ensure that the steering and front-end traction capabilities for Jimmie Johnson's No. 84 Toyota always function at optimal capacity. Racecars traveling at 180 miles per hour in extreme temperatures and ever-changing track conditions, however, require that mechanics know what to tweak when a driver says their car is too tight or too loose. And just like maintaining a race-car's alignment over the course of a race can require frequent adjustments, Ryan says his life as a Christian over the years has required recalibrations of grace and forgiveness to keep him moving in the direction that God has set for him.

As a middle schooler, Ryan professed his faith in Christ at First Baptist Church in Wichita Falls, Texas. For years, he and his younger brother rode the church bus on Sundays and Wednesdays. In high school, Ryan excelled in basketball, but ever since his sophomore year his passion was working on racecars at nearby Red River Raceway. So, when he graduated from high school, he turned down multiple college basketball scholarships to enroll at Ford's mechanic school where he became a master mechanic. Meanwhile, Ryan and his high school sweetheart, Nicole, had a son in 2002 when they were 18.

After graduating from mechanic school and moving to Charlotte in 2005, Ryan landed a job with Roush Fenway Racing as a shop mechanic for NASCAR Hall of Fame driver Mark Martin. Nicole and their son, Jayden, joined Ryan a few months later, and the couple celebrated their fresh start together by getting married. In 2007, the couple's daughter, Kynlee, was born.

Over the course of his career, Ryan has also worked as a gasman and mechanic with several race teams, including Richard Petty Motorsports and JR Motorsports. Being a part of Greg Biffle's 2007 Cup Series win at Kansas Speedway and Noah Gragson's run of 13 Xfinity Series victories between 2020 and 2022 are Ryan's proudest moments of his career. In 2012, Ryan's friend, Xfinity Series driver Justin Allgaier, invited him to attend a prerace chapel service sponsored by Motor Racing Outreach. "I've been a total wreck in the past," Ryan admits." I've been a wreck to my wife and our relationship. I've been given many chances with God's forgiveness."

In May 2015, Ryan was baptized at a public park in a mobile baptism unit as part of MRO's Family Fun Day. He says, "I felt refreshed, like it was a new start. I felt like I could start from there and just move forward in life. I was able to show all those around that Jesus is my Lord and I'm not ashamed." He had wrestled with shame and guilt for years. "I would just beat myself down for the things I've done. But God spoke to me through Psalm 25:20, kind of told me, 'Hey, don't beat yourself up. I'm here for you to help you go forward and not backwards.'" That verse says, "Oh, guard my soul, and deliver me! Let me not be put to shame, for I take refuge in you." The Scripture resonated with Ryan so much that he had it tattooed on his arm along with many other tattoos, including one of a cross and thorns. In describing the image, he says, "It's like an old, tattered scroll. It's got the Bible verse on there, and I've got the cross with the thorns laid over it and it exemplifies that every day I'm praying and thanking God. That's a reminder that He died for our sins. Every tattoo I have has a story or a reason. To be able to talk to people about it, it's been pretty neat."

Ryan says he grew the most in his relationship with Jesus during a mission trip to Haiti in 2016 following the devastating earthquakes in that region. The poverty and desperate need he encountered on the trip humbled him like nothing he had ever experienced before. "At the end of every night, we would circle up around on this rooftop," he recalls. "I'm sitting there and I'm just kind of praying, thanking God for the experience and praying for the people that we saw—that they can get help, that they get nourished, that they get the things they need. And then it came to my turn to talk and I couldn't get a word out. I couldn't get one word out. That was the first time that I felt like I was allowing the Holy Spirit to work in me. I was praying with purpose for those people. It wasn't one of the things that I was needing a favor or anything like that. I thought what I was praying for was going to get answered for those people. And it was just a moment of joy. I was sitting there crying my eyes out."

In sharing about that experience, Ryan testifies, "I was on that rooftop in Haiti with that group of people and I really felt connected with God. I use that point from that day forward to really try to take up my cross as much as I can. I took more away from those trips than I could have ever given any one person on those trips."

Anthony Alfredo

Not for Sale

IN 2023, Xfinity Series driver Anthony Alfredo finished 20th in the championship points standings driving the No. 78 Chevrolet Camaro for BJ McLeod Motorsports. But the Connecticut native has already topped a distinguished list that includes former NASCAR Cup Series champions Joey Logano and Kyle Busch. His 31 endorsement deals that same year leads the pack among NASCAR drivers across the Truck, Xfinity, and Cup Series levels of competition.[1] Anthony's ability to attract advertisers is a highly coveted skill in a sport where sponsorships are the proverbial switch to flip before a driver can answer the call "Start your engines!"

"Everyone told me that early on I would have to build a brand and build my own partnerships if I wanted to go compete, because no matter how much someone liked you, they weren't going to pay for you to drive their car," Anthony says. "There's more opportunity like that in the Cup Series still because that's kind of where the race team business does better. But the lower series are less sustainable for the business owners. That's why you see the bigger Xfinity teams are all owned or affiliated with Cup teams because they're able to multipurpose some of that income. So, it's hard to get your foot in the door without bringing the funding. It's like a pay-to-play sport. So, I have to dedicate a lot of my time to finding sponsors and money to race because without it I won't even go to the track race weekend. I'm 100 percent focused on driving, but during the week I'm 100 percent focused on the business."

As much as Anthony is dependent on sponsorships to live his lifelong dream, his criteria for advertisers on his racecar is nonnegotiable. His Christian witness is not for sale. In 2023, Anthony ended a partnership with one of his major sponsors when one of their marketing campaigns failed to align with his biblical and moral convictions. "That was hard to have to walk away from," he says. "But I have more amazing things or opportunities lined up in 2024 that I may not have had if we didn't make that decision. God works in mysterious ways like that."

Anthony adds, "We have a lot of amazing partners and I am fortunate to work with great people. It is important to me to have sponsors that align with my Christian beliefs and morals for a multitude of reasons. I wouldn't want to represent something I don't believe in, and I don't want my fans or supporters to think I am advocating something that truly doesn't align with my morals."

For Anthony, being conscientious about his public image is driven more by his desire to honor God than building his brand to attract corporate sponsorships. In July 2023, he publicly professed his faith in Christ by being baptized in the ocean at Daytona Beach with about 10 other people who work in NASCAR. The baptismal service was held on a race weekend at sunrise and was led by chaplains with Motor Racing Outreach. "I was born Roman Catholic and baptized at birth, but obviously that wasn't believer's baptism," Anthony says. "I wanted to take that step of publicly declaring my faith and following the Lord." Emily, at that time Anthony's fiancée, had been baptized earlier that same year. Her public profession of faith in Jesus got him to contemplate doing the same. Anthony says, "She didn't really grow up religious at all. Actually, when we met, she had just kind of gotten into it on her own, which I thought was fascinating because I didn't know anyone else who had pursued a faith journey on their own."

Anthony and Emily were married in January 2024. They had met about six years earlier while attending the University of North Carolina at Charlotte. "She and I have been on a pretty awesome faith journey together," he says. "We want to be able to raise our future kids to understand the Word of the Lord and live out their faith in Christ." Anthony thanks God for Emily's faithful example of living for Christ and encouraging him in his daily walk with the Lord. "Every single race, she writes me a prayer that I put in the pocket of my fire suit. She keeps me levelheaded and doesn't let the highs get too high and the lows get too low. She always reminds me that God's got a plan. She's just a super positive person, and she's taught me a lot about life and faith and what it means to be not just a good person but a good Christian."

During his childhood, Anthony's NASCAR idols were Dale Earnhardt Jr., Carl Edwards, and Jimmie Johnson. He says, "They were super successful, but they were really cool guys, at least from what I saw on TV." Anthony's passion for pursuing a career in NASCAR accelerated when he got to drive a late model stock car owned by JR Motorsports. "When I was 17, I got to drive for Dale Jr.'s late model team. Josh Berry and I were teammates and that kind of put me on the map. I won three races that year and finished second to Josh for the championship. At that point in time, I was like, 'Holy cow, I'm driving for my childhood hero.'"

For the 2024 NASCAR season, Anthony reunited with Our Motorsports to drive the No. 5 Chevrolet Camaro full-time in the Xfinity Series. In 2022 he finished 15th in the championship points standings with the same team. Anthony also competes part-time in the Cup Series, driving the No. 62 Chevrolet Camaro for Beard Motorsports. In 2021 he competed full-time in the Cup Series with Front Row Motorsports and finished that season as runner-up for the Sunoco Rookie of the Year.

Starting the 2024 season, Anthony was still pursuing that elusive first victory at any of the top three levels of NASCAR. He says, "The hardest part about racing to accept is there's so much out of your control. You can run the perfect race and blow a tire or something breaks. Or you get wrecked or whatever. And it's so frustrating. It's so hard to stay positive. And I think I've learned to just be a little more patient. But I will not let the ups and downs of racing define me or my life. I think that's something faith has taught me. There's so much more to life than just racing, even though in our industry we sleep and breathe it. And I think those tough times, when you feel like there's nothing else you could have done, that's what has taught me to accept that God has a plan. This is what I've dreamed of doing and always wished I'd be in this position. But it's still humbling, because every day I'm just so thankful for the opportunity."

31

Steve Post

A Racing Heart

FOR NEARLY 40 YEARS, Steve Post has chased his love for motor racing, and that passion has produced several full-circle moments along the way. His fervor for stock car racing seemingly has no limits. From dirt tracks to asphalt, short tracks to superspeedways, ovals to road courses, Steve's boundless energy is full throttle whether he is talking about go-karts, bandolero cars, legend cars, sprint cars, late models, trucks, Xfinity, or Cup Series racing. Growing up in the little town of Hallstead in northeastern Pennsylvania, about six miles from the New York state line, Steve did two things religiously: he went to church morning and night on Sundays and again on Wednesday nights, and he visited the local dirt track on Fridays and Saturdays in season. He recalls, "My dad and I, we would go to dirt track races every Friday night, every Saturday night. My favorite thing to do was always to be at the racetrack. I always loved it. Still to this day I love it."

As a child, when Steve played with his Matchbox cars, he did so with a purpose, creating racetrack scenarios and narrating over the action—a foreshadowing of his future in NASCAR broadcasting. At age 12, he professed his faith in Christ during a revival service at church, where he also sang in the choir and participated in Christmas and Easter drama productions. During high school, Steve volunteered as the public address announcer for the seasonal sports programs, including basketball, wrestling, and volleyball. While a student at Penn State University, he realized an accounting major was the wrong choice, so he switched to marketing. After graduating from college in 1986, Steve worked as a traveling sales rep for a carpet and flooring company, but his real fulfillment came from being the PA announcer at short-track races across northeastern Pennsylvania.

Steve's first full-circle moment occurred when he began announcing races, handling media relations, and editing the program book at Penn Can Speedway in Susquehanna—the same short track he had attended as a child with his father. He also wrote freelance articles for short-track racing trade publications in the Northeast just to get press access at the racetracks. His first radio experience came as an overnight disc jockey for a country station. But as Steve's hobbies became more fulfilling, his day job became more frustrating. Then, while Steve was driving on a work trip one day in the early 1990s, a radio announcer's comments inspired a paradigm shift in his way of thinking. Steve remembers the person saying, "Figure out what you want to do for a living and find some way to do it." That was a light bulb moment for him, and he began thinking, "No, I don't want to be slinging carpet samples around northeastern Pennsylvania."

In 1995, Steve moved to Charlotte for a job as an account manager with a public relations agency—only to discover they hadn't actually secured the account he had been hired to manage. Undeterred, Steve pitted, figuratively speaking, and began volunteering with the media relations team at Charlotte Motor Speedway (CMS). Before long, he landed a job as a public relations representative for NASCAR driver Kenny Wallace. A couple of years later, he moved on to represent Ricky Rudd who drove the No. 28 Ford Taurus for three seasons in the Cup Series with Robert Yates Racing. When Ricky won his first race with RYR at Pocono Raceway north of Allentown, it was another full-circle moment for Steve, who grew up attending races there with his family. Looking back on that time in his life, Steve says, "We won a race at Pocono, won a race at Sonoma and also at Richmond, and it was just wonderful to be at the top of the sport and to see a team form like they did. It was some really good times for Ricky, and it was fun to be part of that, for sure."

Just when Steve seemed to be getting ahead in his public relations career, he again fell to the back of the pack when Ricky left RYR to race for another team, leaving Steve without a job. But it wasn't a dead end for Steve's career. Instead, it was a detour that opened the door for an audition as a pit reporter with Motor Racing Network. That initial 15-race radio broadcast schedule for 2003 only paid $12,000. So, to help provide for his family, Steve worked a number of side jobs, including as PA announcer at CMS, writing for stock car trade magazines, and managing hospitality events for NASCAR driver Jeff Gordon. Now, more than 20 years later, Steve has become a fixture on the MRN broadcast. He is also the PA announcer for the Summer Shootout Series at CMS that features young aspiring racecar drivers. And he hosts the wildly popular *Winged Nation* digital broadcast and covers sprint car racing on MAVTV. "It goes back to my roots, and I just love it," Steve says. Another full-circle moment.

For about 10 years Steve cohosted *NASCAR Performance Live*, a radio program with legendary pit crew chief Larry McReynolds. He credits that experience with helping him build strong relationships with pit crew chiefs and teams in the garage and says it has improved his NASCAR reporting exponentially. He's also thankful for his broadcast mentors in the industry, particularly three whom he had personal friendships with for years. During some of his stints as PA announcer at CMS, Steve worked alongside the late Ken Squier, who cofounded MRN and also served as the lap-by-lap commentator for NASCAR on CBS from 1979 to 1997 and on TBS from 1983 to 1999. The late Barney Hall, known as "the voice of MRN," mentored Steve as well. And Steve continues to stay in touch with Eli Gold, the radio voice of the Alabama Crimson Tide football team. "There are probably eight or 10 of us in the world that make a living doing radio broadcasting of stock car racing," Steve says. "I feel like the whole trajectory of my career—from the short-track stuff to my radio DJ experience in Binghamton, New York—just having all of that experience was God's alignment to get me to where I needed to be. Even going back to my voice, God gave me it all."

Looking back on his career, Steve's most memorable highlight to date is another full-circle moment. In 2021, MRN assigned him the victory lane interview at the Daytona 500 for the first time. The winner of that race was Michael McDowell, a journeyman driver for more than a decade who had never before won a NASCAR Cup Series race. Ten years earlier, Steve had accompanied Michael on several speaking engagements at churches across the country where Michael shared his testimony of his faith in Christ. At those events, Steve would usually host a Q&A session with Michael right before Michael delivered his keynote address, and the two brothers in Christ had developed a strong friendship over the years. Steve says that seeing Michael climb out of his racecar and take hold of the checkered flag as a Daytona 500 champion is a moment he will cherish forever. And when Michael broke the COVID distancing protocols to give Steve a huge hug, he didn't know if he would be able to keep it together emotionally for the interview. "To have the opportunity to ask Michael about that race and hear him break it down is something I'll remember for the rest of my life," he says.

Off the track, Steve is most proud of raising two daughters as a single dad following his unfortunate divorce. His MRN job took him away from home on the weekends, but it also afforded him a lot of quality time during the week with his daughters, who are now both adults. More recently, Steve has been improving his health and fitness by losing more than 50 pounds and running in half-marathons. He says his routine of intermittent walking and jogging has also given him more time to focus on his relationship with God. "Day in and day out, I live in a very noisy world, and my running time gives me a chance to have some alone time with God." Steve points to Matthew 6:33 as one of his favorite Bible verses: "But seek first the kingdom of God and his righteousness, and all these things will be added to you." Those words remind him of how God remains faithful even in the times Steve hasn't been faithful. "It's a blessing that I'm able to be where I'm at," he says.

32

Paul Swan

Lead with Love

GROWING UP NEAR MILWAUKEE, WISCONSIN, Paul
Swan was a four-sport athlete in school, excelling in football,
basketball, baseball, and track. From 2009 to 2013, he played
college football at Bowling Green State University just south
of Toledo, Ohio. He was a three-year starting middle line-
backer and a two-year team captain. In Paul's senior year, the
Falcons won the Mid-American Conference championship.
When he didn't make the cut at an NFL tryout, the exercise
science major enrolled in an internship at Wake Forest University to become a strength and conditioning coach. That's
where he learned about NASCAR's efforts to recruit former
college athletes to work on pit crews. Paul says he thought
that sounded like a great way to still be a competitor and be

on a team, to make a good living, have some fun, and meet some cool people. So he was all for it.

Paul joined Richard Childress Racing in 2014 to help with the organization's strength and conditioning program for its pit crews. After working on pit crews in the Xfinity Series, he was promoted in 2017 to be the tire carrier on the six-member crew for RCR's No. 3 Chevrolet driven by his best friend, Austin Dillon, who would win the Daytona 500 in 2018.

Shortly after Paul came to work at RCR, he and Austin became fast friends. He says, "I met Austin, and we played basketball together, and we played well together. So, we started being on the same team." After the games, Paul and Austin would hang out with their friends, and by 2015 they were housemates. "Austin is the most competitive person I've ever met. I'm very competitive. But he competes at almost everything." As competitive as they both are, Paul and Austin's friendship is rooted in their love for God and their shared passion for boldly living their faith. And it certainly helps that their wives were best friends and in love with Jesus before Austin and Paul came into their lives.

As the story goes, Austin invited his future wife, Whitney, and her best friend, Mariel, to watch him race in Kentucky in 2015. The two women, however, thought they had been invited to the Kentucky Derby, not a NASCAR race. Needless to say, they were surprised and confused when they got to the track and the only horsepower to be found was under the hood of the racecars. Little did they know that weekend would change all their lives, as Paul and Mariel met for the first time as well. Austin and Whitney started dating, and the four friends quickly became inseparable. About eight months later, Paul and Mariel took their friendship to the next level and also started dating. By 2017, the Dillons had tied the knot, and the Swans followed suit in 2019.

The two couples' affinity for spending time together became a major storyline in USA Network's reality television show *Austin Dillon's Life in the Fast Lane*, which followed the four of them during the 2022 Cup Series as they opened their lives to the world. "I really loved being in front of a camera," Paul says. "I have a pretty big personality, and I like to show that personality and have a lot of fun doing it. Just doing life with Mariel, Austin and Whitney, and our families I think is the most fun part. Just being ourselves and having a blast together and showing the world what friendship and love is really about and also intertwining our faith by showing that we're doing all this stuff and having fun, but we also have a very strong faith in God."

Paul had become a Christian during college through the ministry of Fellowship of Christian Athletes and attended small group Bible studies with some of his teammates. But he credits Mariel, a former cheerleader with the Tennessee Titans and a graduate of Middle Tennessee State University, with helping him grow deeper in his relationship with Christ even before they started dating. "We really became best friends, and Mariel's faith is so strong," Paul says. "I admire her faith so much and the person that she is and the love that she has for God. She is literally the best person I know. We both said to each other we're not going to have sex until we get married. And I think it was one of the greatest things I could have done in my life and for our relationship because we got to know each other on a more personal level."

One of Paul's greatest areas of spiritual growth that has made a tremendous impact on his life since he got married is prayer. "I used to pray here and there but never really talked to God, never really made it a point to open up to Him. And I got to the point, where I still do it to this day, is I get on my hands and knees every night before I go to bed, and I pray to God about the good and the bad things. I talk about my goals and aspirations and things I want to accomplish, things I want to fix in my life, things I need help with, and others' needs as well. It feels really good to do that." Paul says that he has learned a lot from Mariel's mother, who is a minister, about how to practically live out his faith. "People are going to mess up and slip up. And they don't need us to fault them for that, they just need to be led to the truth with love and grace." That's why Paul's favorite Bible passage is John 3:16–17: "For God so loved the world, that he gave his only Son, that whoever believes in him should not perish but have eternal life. For God did not send his Son into the world to condemn the world, but in order that the world might be saved through him."

He says, "I can relate to a lot of different people and show people that being a Christian doesn't mean that you're perfect. Everybody messes up and I think there's a stigma around Christians and Christianity in the world's eyes that you have to be perfect to be accepted and you have to do things a certain way to be accepted. I like to make people feel comfortable talking about their faith and their views. If they don't feel comfortable talking about something, great. And if they do, then I'm all ears. I try to be very relatable to people about my faith and where they are in their journey. And when they want to talk about something, I pray that they can feel comfortable talking to me about it. It's crazy what can happen in life when you just put your faith in God."

As a husband and now a father of daughter, Bella Victoria, Paul has a purpose in life bigger than anything he could have imagined. "It's so special to see my relationship with Mariel grow on a daily basis now that we have a daughter in our life. When Bella was born, she just stole my heart immediately. Like, it's crazy how hard I fell in love with her. Being a dad is the best thing in the world." And fatherhood has also strengthened Paul's faith. "That's God's creation," he says of Bella. "And everything around us, He created all this. I pray every night that God will give me the strength to be the best dad I can be, the best husband, and provide for my family and protect them."

And until God leads elsewhere, Paul says he hopes to continue being the tire carrier for RCR's No. 3 Chevrolet. "It's definitely something I want to do as long as I can. I know a lot of guys have been doing this for a long time and you've got to keep your body in shape. So, I'd love to keep doing this and meeting new people and making new relationships while pointing people to Christ."

Susan Chastain

A Mother's Pride and Joy

ROSS CHASTAIN'S METEORIC RISE to NASCAR promi-
nence in 2022 seemingly came out of nowhere. Like when
he drove into the Turn 3 wall at Martinsville Speedway in late
October and accelerated as he rode the barrier to the finish
line and a berth into the Championship 4 round of the Cup
Series playoffs. The driver of Trackhouse Racing Team's No. 1
Chevrolet Camaro ZL1 advanced from 10th position to finish
the race in fifth place with his video game–like maneuver on
the track. "I thought the wall was straight and actually when
you turn into the corner if you look down the backstretch, it
actually goes to the right just a little bit, a couple of inches,"
Ross said. "So when I made the first impact, I thought I was
stopping the way it hit so hard. And I held on to the wheel for

a little bit of time, the best I can remember and then I thought, 'Just let go.' When I let go, my arms got pinned to the right . . . and at that point, I'm like, 'Just don't lift.' All I focused on was making sure my foot didn't come off the gas pedal and I felt like I was going faster than I ever went before."[1]

Ross's unprecedented move on the track has been dubbed the "Hail Melon"—a tribute to his watermelon farming roots—and NASCAR officials proceeded to outlaw it from competition. While competitors and fans alike were awed by it, Ross's biggest fan had a different take. Susan Chastain, Ross's mom, was more philosophical about her son's fearless competitiveness and opportunistic way of always trying to make the most of his chances for success.

For about a decade, Ross bounced around from one race team to another as a backup driver across the Craftsman Truck Series and Xfinity Series while occasionally getting a Cup Series start. "He's always been like, 'I'll drive for anybody, even if it's one race. I just want to drive,'" Susan recalls. And in what can be an emotionally volatile sport, a driver's split-second decisions can have ramifications on and off the track. Even before Ross's jaw-dropping pass on the last lap of that race, his aggressive driving style had made him somewhat of a lightning rod. This was evidenced by the outpouring of both praise and ridicule that seemed evenly split following his high-risk, high-reward decision. Ross had stolen the headlines from the NFL's stranglehold on media coverage and put NASCAR front and center on the television networks and social media video reels.

When Susan was invited to lead the invocation before the race at Darlington Raceway on Mother's Day 2023, she was grateful for the opportunity to pray publicly for the safety of all the drivers and race teams competing against one another. She says, "It was quite an honor to represent all the moms out there." Ross was in contention for the lead for most of the race; however, during a restart with six laps remaining, he lined up alongside Kyle Larson and nudged him up the track. That wrecked both cars and earned Ross a 29th-place finish, while Kyle ended up in 20th. And although Ross didn't drive into victory lane that day, Susan is immensely thankful to have been a part of her son's stop-and-go journey in NASCAR, especially being there when he won his first Cup Series race in 2022 on a road course in Texas.

Since Ross's 2011 debut in the Camping World Truck Series race at Lucas Oil Indianapolis Raceway Park, he has made more than 500 starts across NASCAR's three national series. It took him nine years and 66 tries to finally earn his first of several Truck Series wins. His first Xfinity Series win came after 132 tries over five seasons. And only after 121 starts spread out over six years would he claim his first Cup Series win at Circuit of the Americas in Austin, Texas, on March 27, 2022.

Susan was all smiles as Ross became the 201st different driver to win a Cup race in the history of the sport. And he readily acknowledged his mother during the postrace press conference: "My mom is here, and she's just supported me the whole way. That was the closest I came to crying after the race and just now just thinking about how she doesn't get to come to as many as she wants to. She's a traveling nurse, so she's working an assignment now in North Georgia doing what she wants to do, right? She likes to take care of people, and she wants to save lives, and she's worked through COVID and never backed down and has actually saved lives. For her to take time out of her schedule to come and to work her work schedule around to be here, it's not lost on me."[2]

Ross comes from Alva, Florida, and his family are eighth-generation watermelon farmers who have been involved in the agriculture industry for over a century. The Chastains manage thousands of acres in South Florida that produce more than 2,000 watermelons per acre. The work can be grueling, hot, and intense. Through his teenage years, Ross was either helping around the farm or racing at local short tracks. When Ross's dad, Ralph, started putting him to work as a kid, it was behind the wheel of one of the sawed-off school buses they use to transport melons or driving a tractor rigged to plow or grade land. And Susan remembers that Ross often would have his foot in the throttle, seeking to beat whoever was doing the same job a few rows over.

Susan says that raising a family on the watermelon farm nurtured a determination and strong work ethic that has driven Ross to persevere and refuse to settle for anything less than his best. Susan and Ralph's younger son, Chad, competes part-time in the Craftsman Truck Series and works as a spotter for some of his big brother's Cup races. Susan says that Ross is proud of his nickname "Melon Man" and his family's heritage in the watermelon farming industry. For generations, Chastains have worked six days a week and on Sundays they rested. And Ross could be found parked in front of the television to watch his hero Jeff Gordon battle rivals on the racetrack.

Susan recalls that when Ross was 12 years old and started racing at local short tracks, the family had no expectations other than an entertaining hobby. She never imagined that her once shy child would celebrate after each Cup Series victory by smashing a watermelon on the front stretch. From driving Ross to school and soccer matches when he was a child to watching him discover his passion in motorsports, Susan says there's no doubt he has some God-given abilities when it comes to driving a racecar—kind of like a musician who plays by ear or a person who is naturally mechanical. "Honestly, it's like a gift. I don't say that lightly." Nowadays, Susan is usually there to pick up Ross at the airport when he returns home from traveling the NASCAR circuit. And as good as the victory celebrations are, she's also been there for the disappointments—like when his primary Xfinity Series sponsor was exposed in 2018 for operating a Ponzi scheme. Susan admits, "He's had some heartbreak and some deals fall through. But he never gave up, he never ever quit."

Susan credits the Christian fellowship with like-minded believers that she finds in the Motor Racing Outreach community as a stabilizing force in her life, especially when the noise in the media gets too loud. "My Christian faith is strong," she says, "but living it sometimes is a little more difficult. So, I try to put myself around good people and attend MRO's chapel service when I'm at the race on Sundays. I've got to be good friends with all those guys and their wives, and so you build that network of accountability and support around you." She tries to live a life of gratefulness and always recognize God's many blessings in her life. One of which, she says, is being a mom. "Behold, children are a heritage from the LORD, the fruit of the womb a reward" (Ps. 127:3).

34

Ray Wright

Redeeming the Time

ON RAY WRIGHT'S OFFICE WALL at Richard Childress Racing headquarters hangs a framed photo of "The Catch," Ray's perfectly timed leap to snag a would-be three-run homer at the right-field wall in the 2000 College World Series championship game. Immortalized in the hearts and minds of Louisiana State University fans, that catch preserved LSU's two-run lead over Stanford in the game's third inning. The Tigers from Baton Rouge went on to win the game 6-5 for the program's fifth national title in 10 seasons. For Ray, the photo is more than "glory days" memorabilia. It's a reminder of all the hard work he put in during that season to become an outfielder after being an infielder his entire career.

Ray grew up in an Italian Catholic home where his parents taught him right from wrong, but he attended a private school affiliated with Riverdale Baptist Church in Upper Marlboro, Maryland, to play on their competitive baseball team. Ray recalls, "I go to chapel at Riverdale Baptist and I remember hearing stories from the Bible that I'd never heard before. I had an interaction with the Holy Spirit. I'm under conviction and I'm crying over my sin." When he had a similar experience during a summer youth camp, Ray prayed to receive Jesus as his Savior and Lord. But he admits it was some time before he lived faithfully for Christ. "As I got older, I really didn't take too many strides. I had a one-way relationship with Christ, like, if the sun was in my eyes in the outfield, I would pray, 'Lord, please don't let the baseball hit me out here.' Then, later on that night, if I was with a good-looking woman, I wouldn't be thinking about honoring Jesus."

After college, when Ray's playing days ended after a few years of competing in a semipro independent baseball league, he became a strength coach to help athletes maximize their potential. In 2008, RCR hired him to do exactly that. Ray also worked as a rear tire changer before becoming pit crew manager in 2015. Before going to RCR, Ray had been the strength coach and assistant baseball coach at Forsyth Country Day School where Austin and Ty Dillon, Richard Childress's grandsons, attended and played baseball.

Ray engages his job as RCR's pit crew manager with the same dogged determination that made him stand out among the 15 players in that college championship game who were drafted by Major League Baseball. And as important as physical conditioning is to be the best pit crew in NASCAR, Ray is equally passionate about his team's spiritual health. "This is a very aggressive sport," he says. "This is a very aggressive business. People take advantage of you. You've got to do your best to be tough and hard-nosed, while also being genuine and sincere about caring for the people you work with. I think my guys know I'm sincere and that I honestly do care about them."

A regulation NASCAR pit crew has five over-the-wall members—tire carrier, two tire changers, jackman, and gasman—and five behind-the-wall members. Pit crew members usually do not perform mechanical work on the cars. They often fly into the race location the morning of the event and return home immediately following the race. "You got to have some athleticism," Ray says. "That's the only physical attribute. You've got to be able to be mentally strong. We recruit former college athletes because they've had to deal with constructive criticism. They've overcome adversity. They've handled failure. That's all this sport is. It's a cliché, but it's really 90 percent mental. But you got to have the physical presence to do that as well."

And if you're wondering what excellence looks like on pit road now that the Next Gen racecars have only one lug nut instead of five, Ray says that the benchmark to avoid losing position on the racetrack is under 10 seconds for four tires and fuel. Working on a pit crew demands the ultimate teamwork to be successful, as the team members depend on each other to be in sync as a group. Ray says it's the same idea as the apostle Paul's description of how the church should work together as the body of Christ. "The hand needs the arm, the toes need the feet, the feet need the leg. It all works together."

Ray is especially burdened for what he describes as a lack of biblical manhood and masculinity being taught in most churches. "I feel like it's so overlooked," he says, "and I feel like that's why men are scarce in the church." Jesus's humanity, although He is also fully God, Ray says, is a picture of Christ that men should be encouraged by. That's one of the reasons he paid to see *The Passion of the Christ* about eight times when the movie debuted in theaters in 2004. "I remember that part where the actor who [played] Jesus looked in the camera and said, 'When the world hates you, remember it hated me first.' How many times did Christ drop his cross? Like we're going to drop our cross. We've just got to pick it up again and get going, and we're given the grace to do it."

But Ray says that whatever shortcomings the church may have in relating to men, it's still their responsibility to study the Scriptures personally and learn about the type of man Jesus was during his time on earth. "I can't emphasize enough that men need to do the work for themselves. They need to pick up a Bible and they need to educate themselves on who Jesus is. They need to be a man and accept accountability. Because when you educate yourself on who Christ is, you can't blame others for being hypocritical in their faith. That's a cop-out. Men have been copping out for too long. They need to accept accountability for themselves and their household."

For Ray, one of the best biblical examples of a man being accountable and responsible for his actions is David. He singlehandedly took on the giant Goliath and the Philistine army. "I feel like David was a dude," Ray says. "David made mistakes and fell on his face, but he never quit loving God. Why would you not want that guy on your team? And those prophets back in the day were hardcore for God. You could go through the whole Bible and find great stuff about men of God." It's important to Ray that his wife and four teenage children see that he strives, albeit imperfectly, to be a man after God's own heart. "I'm not trying to act like my life's perfect," he says. "But no matter how things go, Christ is always the cornerstone of my life and the foundation of my life."

About 10 years ago, Ray was compelled to be more intentional about sharing God's love in his community. He says, "We had a Bible study at work, and it occurred to me that we're just meeting in a room talking about being holy and reading the same Bible verses, but when we got out of that room, nothing was really changing." John 13:34 has become Ray's mission in life: "A new commandment I give to you, that you love one another: just as I have loved you, you also are to love one another." That's why he started a charity called Pit Stops for Hope. "Christ says people will know your mindset by how you love one another. So, being the very privileged person that I am," Ray admits, "I didn't know what problems are in the area. So I Google searched 'problems in North Carolina' and it came up with child food insecurity. We started raising money for Second Harvest Food Bank." Pit Stops for Hope has since expanded to helping provide schools with resources to assist children and families mired in poverty, "and hopefully, the Holy Spirit is going to take care of the rest," he says.

35

Jerry Caldwell

The Blessing of Adoption

AS PRESIDENT AND GENERAL MANAGER of Bristol Motor Speedway (BMS), Jerry Caldwell has overseen some spectacular transformations at the stadium-like structure that houses a .533-mile concrete oval with a pair of 650-foot straightaways. In recent years, the historic venue, surrounded by the scenic mountains of northeast Tennessee near the Virginia state line, has taken NASCAR back to its roots by converting to a dirt track for one of its two yearly races. And there's no better place to watch America's Night Race than after dark at BMS. The 500-plus-acre complex—also known as the World's Fastest Half-Mile, Thunder Valley, and the Holy Grail of Short Tracks—includes a quarter-mile drag strip and schedules about 150 events each year, including festivals and concerts by some of the world's premiere musical artists.

It's no wonder then that Jerry was recognized in 2023 as Tennessee Tourism Leader of the Year, the ultimate recognition from the state's hospitality and tourism industry. "We're called to do things in an excellent manner," Jerry says. "Let's serve people well. Let's love on folks and allow them to come have an experience and create lasting memories with their families. And we're blessed to be able to do that." For Jerry, that's what life is all about—family and transforming lives. And both are inextricably connected to his nearly three-decade career at BMS.

Jerry attended King University, a small private Christian school, on a golf scholarship. During his senior year in 1997, the business finance major did an internship in the events department at the speedway in nearby Bristol, Tennessee. After graduation, Jerry turned down a job offer from a bank in Memphis to go to work full-time in the sales department at the racetrack. He says, "God gave me wisdom enough to know that at the end of the day, this whole journey is about people and relationships. It's really important to be around good people. And I knew that these were good folks that I worked with. I enjoyed being with them and kind of going to battle with them, if you will, as we put on events."

After impressing BMS general manager Jeff Byrd with his job skills, Jerry set his sights on impressing his boss's daughter, Belton, who he married in 2001. The couple's vision for their family included having two biological children and then adopting two more. But in 2006, after struggling with infertility for several years, Jerry and Belton decided to go ahead and submit their paperwork to start what is typically an 18-month adoption process. "Who are we to tell God how he's going to bless us?" Jerry says. "And God has blessings for us if we're willing to accept them. It may not be the way that we had dreamed. It may not be the way we have drawn it up. But He has amazing blessings, far greater than we can ask or imagine, if we're open to letting Him write the story."

Surprisingly, the same day that the couple submitted their application, the adoption agency paired them with their son-to-be, Caleb. "God had made it very clear to us," Jerry recalls. "That's our son. This is what we're supposed to do." In early 2008, the couple again applied to adopt, and within two months, two birth moms had selected them as adoptive parents. The Caldwells' daughters, Emma and Bella, were born five weeks apart and were welcomed into the family within 10 days of each other.

While adopting or fostering children may not be for every family, Jerry believes that for Christians it holds special significance. The Bible teaches that Christ-followers are adopted into God's family when they receive His gift of salvation upon professing their faith in the death, burial, and resurrection of Jesus Christ for the forgiveness of their sins. "I think it starts with always remembering that God doesn't make mistakes," he says. "There's one Creator of life, and He chose to put us on this big ball of dirt together for a reason. He designs you exactly the way you are for a reason. It doesn't mean we always make the right choice. And that's where parents come in, and we can help guide and steer our children to thank God for His grace and love and mercy."

And then 2010 happened. Shortly after Jerry was promoted to vice president of sales for the speedway, Jeff Byrd, Jerry's father-in-law and BMS general manager, was diagnosed with a brain tumor. Jerry became interim general manager while Jeff battled valiantly for 10 months, enduring cancer treatments at the finest research medical centers in Houston and New York. Meanwhile, amid this family crisis, the adoption agency called again. And again Jerry and Belton said yes. "So, we got our daughter Lila, who was just a few weeks old, on October 8, and then Jeff died on October 17. It was very much like God giveth and taketh away," he recalls. Belton's mom, Claudia, moved in for a few months to help with the four children, while Jerry transitioned into the general manager role at BMS. Jerry says that Speedway Motorsports, LLC, the owners of the track, were especially supportive in the wake of Jeff's death. "They were the hands and feet of Jesus. They wrapped their arms around us and loved us through it. It was a trying time, but also through that pain and brokenness was a beautiful time of growth. Just seeing God's hand in the mess."

In 2019, God led Jerry and Belton to become foster parents for a nine-month-old boy whose birth mom was also expecting another son. Eighteen months later, after strongly advocating for the children's safety and well-being, the Caldwells adopted both boys. "Again, Jesus is in the midst of broken situations, and so that led to the eventual adoption of biological brothers, our sons Preston and Mack." The Caldwells' experiences compelled them to advocate for better laws and policies to ensure children's safety and to streamline the adoption process for those in the foster care system. Jerry says, "Through the process of some of the broken situations and messed up things that we dealt with, I went to the governor and sat down with him and said, 'This has got to be addressed.' And God used our story along with lots of other stories to have our governor, who's a strong Christian, to say, 'All right, we have to do something about this foster care and adoption situation in Tennessee.' And in 2022, there were several new laws passed, improving that process. It's not perfect but is getting much better."

Jerry says that his passion for family and transforming lives was born out of gratitude for his own Christian upbringing. He made a profession of faith in Christ at age 16 and learned how to grow in his relationship with Jesus during college. "We've also told our kids that your story is your story," he says. "But your story is also your story to share at some point. Because God's written that story for a reason." In 2022, Jerry and Belton shared their adoption story on a prerace show that aired on FOX. "God didn't write the story for us to keep it to ourselves. He's been faithful through this, and He has a plan and He has a purpose. And we can share our story and hopefully it can help somebody else or inspire them or point them closer to God. We've been extremely blessed and continue to be thankful to be able to raise these kids in a loving home that loves the Lord. We want to point our kids towards that and allow them to be salt and light in this world."

36

Billy Mauldin

Knowing Jesus and Lifting Him Up

AS PRESIDENT AND CEO of Motor Racing Outreach for two-and-a-half decades, Billy Mauldin's sure and steady presence amid the organized chaos of race day is like the calm before and after a storm. Although he has never driven a racecar and didn't grow up following racing, he still knows what it's like to pursue dreams and operate in very intense and fast-paced environments. The Charlotte, North Carolina native's career path—from construction site work to youth ministry to state and national politics to motorsports chaplaincy to *American Idol* guru—may not seem like the ideal example of résumé building. But it does make for an adventurous life when God leads the way.

"It a joy to think back on how God has navigated my life," Billy says. "I see now how He worked all of it out to teach and offer insight and preparation for the next assignment. If God calls you to any setting somewhere, He's going to use you to create an impact on people's lives in amazing ways."

That's been a driving passion for Billy ever since his early 20s when he got on his knees in the middle of the day and prayed in the back of a storage unit on a construction job site in Savannah, Georgia. "I just went to the back of this tool trailer and got down on my knees, and I just simply said, 'God, I'm tired of hurting. If You can help me, please help me. Please help me.'" The previous couple of weeks, Billy had spent the evenings after work in his hotel room reading passages his grandmother recommended from his copy of the Children's Living Bible. She also wrote him a letter about trusting God with his life. Billy says he has never been the same since crying out to God for help. "I remember walking out the door and hitting the top of the steps going down from the trailer, and all of a sudden I realized I wasn't alone. And it dawned on me that so much of what I was wrestling with and was struggling with was loneliness. And I realized too that God had done something. I couldn't articulate it. I couldn't frame it, and I couldn't tell you what necessarily, but I knew something had happened."

When Billy returned home from his construction job the following weekend, he attended his home church for the first time since he had stopped going at age 13. "I walked in the back and sat down," he recalls. "And at the end of the service, the pastor gave an altar call for anybody who wants to accept Christ as their Savior and Lord to come forward. And I did just that. A childhood friend of mine who had been in that church when I was a kid came up behind me and met me, and we prayed. And he began to disciple me. The rest of that fall we spent hours and hours together, and he was just pouring into me Scripture, books, and tapes. The Word of God just exploded inside me, and the yearning to know Him more and to be constantly in prayer was all-consuming to my life."

In January of the following year, Billy re-enrolled at Appalachian State University in Boone, North Carolina, where he had dropped out the previous semester lacking purpose and hope. He joined the InterVarsity Christian Fellowship group that met on campus on Tuesday nights. "Next thing you know, within a week or two I had more friends than I'd ever had before," he says. "I was involved in InterVarsity, and going to a local church, and then finding other friends to do small group Bible studies and prayer groups with, and it just became a whole lifestyle. My relationship with the Lord was really far, far more important to me and more of my focus than even my college degree." His studies eventually came into focus. And with a desire to finish well, Billy graduated with a degree in business administration and a minor in international business. For the next several years he worked in commercial and residential construction while his girlfriend, Julie, who he first met through InterVarsity, completed her degree at Appalachian State a couple of years behind him. Three years after she graduated, they got married.

In the early 1990s, Billy left the construction industry to serve as a full-time youth minister for a couple of years before transitioning into politics when a friend connected him with Robin Hayes's gubernatorial campaign. "I spent one session one summer up in Raleigh with [Hayes] because he was also a member of the North Carolina House when he was running for governor, and I got to see behind the scenes how state government works," Billy says. In 1996, he traveled across the state and country as Hayes's special assistant. Although the gubernatorial bid failed, a couple of years later Hayes was elected to serve in the United States House of Representatives.

Billy faced a crossroads in his mid-30s: move to Capitol Hill and dive deeper into the cutthroat world of national politics or accept an invitation to be a chaplain in the competitive, fast-paced world of NASCAR. "This was a very difficult decision at the time," Billy says. Robin had become a very close friend and there were aspects of politics and governing that I really enjoyed." Billy had already served as an MRO chaplain for a boat racing series and had led a Bible study in NASCAR legend Darrell Waltrip's race shop. Every time he served with MRO, it became clearer where God was leading him. So, Billy decided to leave politics and join MRO full-time in 1999.

"Our ministry is mostly about presence," he says. "We go to the tracks and we have a rough idea of what we're planning to do. But once you get there, you then stop and wait and see what needs to be done. God just opens doors for you, and then you respond accordingly. That's why in order to do this type of ministry, you have to be committed to sensing the Holy Spirit's voice and following the Holy Spirit. If you're the kind of person that believes you can put a plan together and then execute the plan, it isn't going to work that way, not in this world."

Billy says that helping people understand the truth of God's Word empowers them to not be deceived and fall victim to Satan's schemes. "Satan tries to get us responding to him versus us responding to the truth and God's Word. And once he gets us responding to him and doing things his way, he can lead us down his dark paths until we recognize what's going on and we start responding again to God's Word and His truth of who we truly are, as He created us to be. The enemy wants to control the narrative and put you on your heels. Jesus has given us victory and the call to share the Good News!"

In addition to his administrative responsibilities, Billy regularly leads prerace chapel services for the race teams and their families to attend on race day, as well as helping host the MRO Community Center where families gather on race weekend. He also leads small group Bible studies, offers invocations, provides counseling, and officiates weddings, and he makes his rounds visiting in the garage and on pit road on race day. Often someone will approach him and ask for prayer or share something they're struggling with. Billy says spiritual conversations usually occur while leaning up against a set of tires in the garage or in the back of the racecar hauler or sitting around a driver's or owner's motor coach. "You quickly have to begin the process of unpacking where someone is spiritually and then trying to just get them into God's Word," he says. In the motorsports world, fame and fortune can be two of the biggest hindrances to people experiencing God's very best for their lives. According to Billy, "That's a lot of the spiritual battle for all of us, whether it's finding our relationship with the Lord, or walking consistently and faithfully with Him."

Having had a career in politics and NASCAR that's placed him on private jets and in green rooms with celebrities, professional athletes, and state and national leaders, Billy wasn't blinded by Hollywood's bright lights in 2014 when the executive producers of *American Idol* invited him and his wife to be spiritual advisers for the show's contestants during Season 13. For four months, from January to April, they made weekly flights to West Hollywood to build relationships with the contestants and encourage them throughout the competition, especially when a contestant was eliminated. "We knew why we were there," Billy says. "We were there for the kids. We stayed behind the scenes and worked with the kids and loved on them and did what we were called to do. We were blessed to be given amazing access to every aspect of the industry and to get to know the tireless staff and Idol family behind the scenes. Even to this day we are still in touch fairly regularly with many of the contestants, including the winner, Caleb Johnson, as well as vocal coaches, producers, and others who made that season happen." After traveling 30-plus race weekends every year while Julie was usually at home caring for their four children, the opportunity for Billy to do ministry alongside his wife was extremely special.

Meanwhile, the daily opportunity to do life alongside the professional NASCAR community requires that Billy first have a daily encounter with Jesus. "My determined purpose is this, that I may know Him deeply, personally, and intimately. I think everything flows out of that. What I have to give or share, or the capacity that I have to serve others with the depth and breadth of my knowing Him and being in relationship with Him. If I focus on my need to know Him, then that enables me to help others know Him. We must all continue to learn to listen to the Holy Spirit and follow His direction and guidance daily. This is where the adventure of faith happens. The place where you become more excited about the unexpected than the planned, where you see God work firsthand in your life and in others. Where peace overwhelms you whether in the storms of life or on the mountaintops. Where you experience the truth of Jesus's words when He promised, 'I will never leave you nor forsake you'" (Heb. 13:5).

ACKNOWLEDGMENTS

Like a 10-month NASCAR race schedule, writing a book is a test of endurance and perseverance. And one thing I've learned about stock car racing from interviewing many of the industry's leaders for this book is that a racecar driver isn't successful without a team of people who share the same goals.

Similarly, the writing of *Sundays at the Track* would have never come to fruition without the contributions and sacrifices of dozens of like-minded people who are passionate about running the race of faith with their eyes on the prize of their upward calling in Christ Jesus.

Special thanks go to NASCAR Hall of Fame driver and three-time Cup Series champion Darrell Waltrip for writing the foreword for the book, as well as to all those who have endorsed this project. Also, thank you to Dan Balow of the Steve Laube Agency for being my literary agent and believing in my vision for this project.

My heartfelt desire to write a book pointing motorsports fans to Christ through personal stories of God's grace and redemption from those who make a living in the fast lane would have remained a dream without the enthusiastic support and partnership of Motor Racing Outreach president and CEO Billy Mauldin. For 25 years, Billy has ministered to the professional NASCAR community and their families by sharing and showing the love of Christ through good times and bad. As a Bible teacher, Christian counselor, and mentor at the highest level of stock car racing, Billy's endorsement and consistent advocacy for this book opened doors for me that I never could have entered on my own. Thank you, Billy, for paving the way so that people around the world can read about God's faithfulness in the lives of some of NASCAR's most celebrated competitors.

Furthermore, I'm extremely appreciative for each of the 36 individuals who trusted me with sharing their faith journeys in this book. Your humility, transparency, and selflessness in acknowledging Jesus as the hero of your story is a true testament of what surrendering one's life to following Christ is all about. Such inspiring and convicting testimonies for God's glory are the embodiment of the apostle Paul's exhortation in 2 Corinthians 1:3–4:

> Blessed be the God and Father of our Lord Jesus Christ, the Father of mercies and God of all comfort, who comforts us in all our affliction, so that we may be able to comfort those who are in any affliction, with the comfort with which we ourselves are comforted by God.

The editorial and marketing teams at Baker Publishing Group supported me and kept me on track like a racing team's championship-caliber pit crew. As senior acquisitions editor, Rachel McRae's steady encouragement, prompt feedback, and insightful direction throughout the writing process proved invaluable for getting this project successfully across the finish line. Also, my manuscript editor, Amy Nemecek, helped make the book read like a finely tuned and well-oiled machine. And many thanks go to Sarah Trail, Hannah Boers, and Rod Jantzen for their marketing and sales expertise.

Finally, I'm grateful to my own home team who has encouraged me throughout this writing journey. My lovely wife, Dawn, and our children, Anna, Lydia, Caleb, and Avery, inspire me every day by their selfless pursuits of God's plans and purposes for their lives. And to that end, may we all continue chasing God's best just like His Word instructs in Philippians 3:13–14:

> Brothers, I do not consider that I have made it my own. But one thing I do: forgetting what lies behind and straining forward to what lies ahead, I press on toward the goal for the prize of the upward call of God in Christ Jesus.

NOTES

Chapter 1 Joe Gibbs

1. Joe Gibbs with Jerry B. Jenkins, *Game Plan for Life* (Carol Stream, IL: Tyndale, 2009), 8.

2. Tom Jensen, "Joe Gibbs Honors His Late Son," NASCAR Hall of Fame, June 21, 2021, https://www.nascarhall.com/blog/joe-gibbs-honors-his-late-son.

Chapter 3 Chase Briscoe

1. Chase Briscoe (@chasebriscoe_14), Instagram, May 20, 2020, https://www.instagram.com/p/CAawv3HBWMg/.

2. "Briscoe Emotional after Darlington Win," NASCAR, YouTube video, May 21, 2020, https://www.youtube.com/watch?v=1tNkqbL7OQg.

3. Steve Samra, "Joe Gibbs Reveals Why He Chose Chase Briscoe to Replace Martin Truex Jr. in 2025," 5GOATS, June 25, 2024, https://www.on3.com/pro/news/joe-gibbs-reveals-why-he-chose-chase-briscoe-to-replace-martin-truex-jr-in-2025/.

Chapter 4 Marcus Smith

1. "Speedway Facts," Charlotte Motor Speedway, accessed June 24, 2024, https://www.charlottemotorspeedway.com/fans/track-facts/.

Chapter 5 Kelley Earnhardt Miller

1. Kelley Earnhardt Miller with Beth Clark, *Drive: 9 Lessons to Win in Business and in Life* (Nashville: W Publishing, 2020), 8–9.

Chapter 7 Aric Almirola

1. Aric Almirola (@Aric_Almirola), X, December 13, 2023, https://twitter .com/Aric_Almirola/status/1734956916202238112.

2. Aric Almirola, "My Baptism: A Day I'll Never Forget!," YouTube, uploaded by Aric Almirola, November 6, 2019, https://www.youtube.com /watch?v=Ban9UWuEUF0.

Chapter 13 Michael McDowell

1. Greg Engle, "2021 NASCAR Daytona 500: Michael McDowell Post Race," YouTube, uploaded by Greg Engle, February 15, 2021, https://www .youtube.com/watch?v=KEoe-VAnYO0.

2. Some of the quoted material in this chapter was previously published in Lee Weeks, "Driven to Glorify God," *Decision*, May 2021, https://decision-magazine.com/driven-to-glorify-god/.

3. Michelle R. Martinelli, "Joey Logano Says He and Teammate Brad Keselowski Haven't Talked About Daytona 500 Wreck, but 'We Will Fix It,'" *For the Win* (blog), February 19, 2021, https://ftw.usatoday.com/2021 /02/nascar-joey-logano-keselowski-penske-daytona-500-wreck.

Chapter 14 Corey LaJoie

1. Samaritan's Feet, "Our Work," SamaritansFeet.org, accessed January 16, 2024, https://samaritansfeet.org/our-work/impact/.

Chapter 18 Bobby and Kristin Labonte

1. NASCAR, "Bobby Labonte HOF Speech," Facebook video, February 1, 2020, https://www.facebook.com/NASCAR/videos/bobby-labonte-hof -speech/539558353330848/.

Chapter 24 Jason Ratcliff

1. "Jason Ratcliff to Serve as Team/Driver Coordinator of Joe Gibbs Racing's Xfinity and ARCA Programs," Jayski's Silly Season Site, November 2, 2023, https://www.jayski.com/2023/11/02/jason-ratcliff-to-serve-as-team -driver-coordinator-of-joe-gibbs-racings-xfinity-and-arca-programs/.

2. Racing Reference Info Site, "Kyle Busch," Racing-referenceinfo.com, accessed February 12, 2024, https://www.racing-reference.info/driver/Kyle _Busch/.

3. "Jason Ratcliff to Serve as Team/Driver Coordinator."

Chapter 25 Chris Rice

1. NASCAR Foundation, "The NASCAR Foundation Announces New Members to Board of Directors," NASCAR.com, April 13, 2023, https://www

.nascar.com/news-media/2023/04/13/the-nascar-foundation-announces
-new-members-to-board-of-directors-2/.

Chapter 27 Jordan Anderson

1. Dustin Long, "Friday 5: Jordan Anderson Recounts Firey Talladega
Crash," NBC Sports, October 28, 2022, https://www.nbcsports.com/nascar
/news/friday-5-jordan-anderson-recounts-fiery-talladega-crash-ryan-blaney
-ross-chastain-chase-elliott-denny-hamlin.

Chapter 30 Anthony Alfredo

1. "Anthony Alfredo, Ryan Vargas Top List for Most Brand Endorse-
ments Among NASCAR Drivers," Outsider.com, May 4, 2023, https://www
.outsider.com/sports/nascar/anthony-alfredo-ryan-vargas-top-list-for-most
-brand-endorsements-among-nascar-drivers/.

Chapter 33 Susan Chastain

1. Kelly Crandall, "Chastain Still in Disbelief 'Hail Melon' Worked at
Martinsville," Racer.com, October 28, 2023, https://racer.com/2023/10/28
/chastain-still-in-disbelief-hail-melon-worked-at-martinsville/.

2. Daniel McFadin, "'Razor's Edge': Ross Chastain & His Mom's Belief
in Him," Frontstretch.com, March 28, 2022, https://frontstretch.com/2022
/03/28/razors-edge-ross-chastain-and-his-moms-belief-in-him/.

LEE WEEKS is an author, journalist, editor, communication strategist, and former senior pastor. He holds a bachelor's degree in journalism and mass communication from the University of North Carolina at Chapel Hill and a master's degree with biblical languages from Southeastern Baptist Theological Seminary, Wake Forest, North Carolina.

Lee is passionate about communicating the life-changing message of the gospel in clear, creative, and compelling ways as expressed in Scripture and exemplified in real-life stories of people who have been transformed by God's redemptive work in their own lives. Learn more at lee-weeks.com.

CONNECT WITH LEE

Lee-Weeks.com

 @lee.weeks.50

 @weeks_lee